Clinical Counseling
and Psychotherapy

Bob H. Frey, Ph.D., Psy.D.

authorHOUSE®

AuthorHouse™
1663 Liberty Drive
Bloomington, IN 47403
www.authorhouse.com
Phone: 1-800-839-8640

First published by AuthorHouse   01/28/2012

ISBN: 978-1-4685-4686-6 (sc)
ISBN: 978-1-4685-4689-7 (ebk)

Printed in the United States of America

Any people depicted in stock imagery provided by Thinkstock are models, and such images are being used for illustrative purposes only.
Certain stock imagery © Thinkstock.

This book is printed on acid-free paper.

CONTENTS

Special Recognition
When Families Are On The Brink
Clayton Center Offers In-Home Help

By Marie Hardin
Clayton News/Daily

Fighting, lying in general misery were all part of the Olvera household.

It was constant fights. "We were at each other's throats all the time," said Barbara Olvera, sitting on a couch in her living room. That was before the doctor paid a house call.

"If it wasn't for Dr. (Bob) Frey, I don't know how we would have survived," said Olvera. She and her family were participants in an in-home crisis therapy program offered through the Clayton Center, an innovative approach that takes therapy straight into the homes of families in trouble.

The program, which started in October thanks to a state grant, has lightened the load for other outpatient therapists with the Clayton Center and spared some Clayton County families the pain of separation, said Frey, psychotherapist and clinical supervisor of the in-home program.

The program was presented to the Olveras as a way to keep their family intact. Olvera knew that Barbara Franks, her 13-year-old daughter, would be removed from the home unless they participated in the counseling.

Franks, who has already been hospitalized, had been diagnosed as severely emotionally disturbed, a qualifying criterion for participation in the program.

Olvera said the family was uncomfortable during the first couple of visits from Frey.

But "after the second visit, Dr. Frey made us feel like he wasn't against what we said." Olvera said. Frey spent an average of four hours a week in the Olvera in the Olvera home for about a three-month period. Frey said family therapy lasts anywhere from four to 16 weeks, depending on the need.

Counselors use brief solution-focused therapy, said Frey, an intensive type counseling which focuses on helping families design solutions to their problems.

Families have to be ready to do their part, he said.

"In order for it to work, they have to want it to work," said Frey.

Like the many families he deals with, Frey said it took a few sessions for the "masking" to stop, and the real business of honesty facing the issues to begin.

"It started turning at that point," he said.

Things are better. So much better, in fact, that on Dr. Frey's last visit, he watched a videotape of Frank's baptism ceremony at the Pinecrest Baptist Church in Morrow.

Frey said he's seen tremendous change in the family dynamic. Things were unmanageable when he began visiting the Olvera family, he said.

That's changed. "The family is interacting as a group." He said. "They've never been able to do that before." Frey said for a family to really succeed in the program, it takes a collaborative effort by family, in-home counselor, and representatives from other community organizations, such as Department of Family and Children Services, the school system or the juvenile court system.

"It's not just the in-home team doing all the work," he said.

For the Olveras, the work done by themselves, Frey and others has had its rewards, Olvera said it had been a long time since family members expressed affection for one another. "I love you" was never heard.

Chapter I

The Parakletos in Counseling

Counseling is one of the great works and missions of God. Effective counseling cannot be accomplished apart from the aid and ministry of the Holy Spirit. In order to heal the hurts of mortal man the Spirit of God must be engaged, and is a vital part of the work involved. It is significant to remember that the Holy Spirit is not a thing or an object and should not be referred to in this manner. He is the third person of the triune Godhead. He is along with God, the Heavenly Father and God, the Son (Jesus), the three in one God. He is in every respect and aspect co-equal with the Heavenly Father and Son. Again, the Holy Spirit should be involved in counseling or else the therapeutic session will be void and empty of any real hope of lasting success. To leave out the Holy Spirit in Counseling is comparable to preaching a sermon, people are regenerated through the blood, but never mentioning whose blood (Christ's) it is that saves us from our sins. Christ promised the coming of the Holy Ghost (Spirit) in the Book of John. (John 14:26)

> But the Comforter, who is the Holy Ghost, whom the Father will send in My name, He shall teach you all things, and bring all things to your remembrance, whatsoever I have said unto you.[1]

The word "Comforter" is from the Greek word "Paraclete" which means counselor. The word also carries the idea of the Holy Spirit as advocate, Dr. Jay Adams writes:

> But there is good reason, however, to translate parakletos in
> its occurrences-in John by "advocate" or intercessor."[2]

The Holy Ghost came in the place of Christ Jesus to be our comforter and counselor. Counselors who do not know Christ as Lord and Savior do not have divine ministry of the Holy Ghost in their counseling. Many of today's secular counselors openly deny the existence of God and depend upon their own futile attempts at solving the troubles of all mankind. This is indeed the "blind leading the blind."

For counseling to be "Christian" it must be carried on in harmony with the regenerating and sanctifying work of God, the Holy Spirit. The Holy Spirit is called, "Holy," because He is God. He is holy in all aspects of His eternal being as is the Heavenly Father and the Son, the Lord Jesus Christ. Through the grace and mercy of God it is possible for the Holy Ghost to impart to believers such traits as (1) gentleness; (2) love; (3) patience; (4) joy; (5) faithfulness; (6) self-control (7) peace (8) kindness (9) goodness; God declares these to be the fruits and results of the work of the Holy Spirit. Galatians 5: 22-23.

It is a futile attempt to try to generate these qualities apart from the Holy Spirit. To attempt this is comparable to open rebellion against God Almighty. Some humanistic counselors even seek to assume the authority of God. In their attempt to bypass the Holy Spirit demonstrates a human depravity and man's attempt to reflect his own goodness apart from God. In the absence of the grace of God, man is left empty and destitute of any virtue. He only has the results of a legalistic work righteousness, which will lead him to despair and more misery. No man can be truly happy apart from his creator. Only God can give peace and completeness to men's lives.

The Holy Ghost is indeed the source of all personality and behavioral changes, that involves a viable relationship to and with God. The Holy Ghost is the one who brings life to the dead sinner lost in his trespasses and sins through the blood of the Lord Jesus

Christ. Christian counselors should return to their Lord and depend upon the Holy Ghost to lead them in counseling. Christian counselors know the answer to what brings peace and happiness in this life. Many Christians turn to secular counselors in time of trouble when they should be seeking the face of God. This reminds us of the words of Apostle Paul in Galatians 3:3:

> Are ye so foolish? Having begun in the Spirit, are ye now made perfect in the flesh?[3]

Yet these Christians will still ask, "Why do not I have peace?" The reason is that they turn to men for answers. These men themselves do not know the Prince of Peace and therefore cannot know the peace of God. How foolish it is when Christian ministers will refer their members and others to be treated, studied and analyzed by non-Christian psychiatrists and or\psychologists who have never been born again by the Spirit of God. How sad it is when God's preachers deliver his people into the hands of ravening wolves.

The Holy Ghost works in the lives of believers through the eternal grace of God. The Holy Spirit uses the scripture, prayer and the fellowship of God's people to bring about changes in people's lives. Secular counseling apart from the spirit of God can never effect permanent changes in the children of men. Perfect change only comes through the mercy and grace of God Almighty.

The problems of secular counseling is felt by almost every God called minister. We are constantly bombarded by propaganda, frustration and expert knowledge from so called experts. We are told that we do not know how to handle the complex troubles of life. The Christian is told to refer his people to the experts who can give him all the secular world has to offer. Christian counselors need to remember those wonderful word of our blessed Savior. Matthew 11: 28-30.

> Come unto Me, all ye that labor and are heavy laden, and I will give you rest. Take my yoke upon you, and learn of me; for I am meek and lowly in heart, and ye shall find rest unto your souls. For my yoke is easy, and my burden is light."[4]

It is time for the Christian counselor to seek forgiveness of God Almighty. We have let the secular counselor rob us of a vital ministry given by the Holy Ghost of God. We need to open our hearts and reexamine our counseling ministry. We need to ask the Spirit of God to give us wisdom to do this great work.

Again, we need to remember the Holy Spirit is God. He has all the attributes of God. He is not the figment of God's imagination, nor is He thought beams of God. He is, as stated previously, the third person of the triune Godhead. He works in complete harmony with the Heavenly Father, and the Son the Lord Jesus. It is God who chooses the times, means, and occasions for working in the lives of people. Christian counselors must respect the sovereignty of the Holy Ghost. The expectations of counselors and clients must all conform to the will and authority of God, the Holy Spirit. Counselors should always search for the guidance and ministry of the Holy Ghost in order to aid the people in whom he serves. This should encourage and not discourage the counselor and client. It should encourage the Counselor and client to know that God's spirit is working to solve their problems.

The counselor's gifts and abilities of the Holy Spirit are exercised under the Spirit's direction. Therefore, the Christian counselor should not be sloppy in the way he conducts his counseling. The Holy Ghost wants a clean vessel in which to operate. Rev. Charles Spurgeon once said that:

> "The Holy Spirit will not use a dirty pitcher to carry the Water of Life."[5]

The Holy Ghost has chosen to work through the human agent, a fact that has been clearly demonstrated through the giving of gifts to the church of God. The Holy Ghost gives gifts to whomsoever He pleases. Some believers have more than one gift, while others only have one gift. God, the Holy Ghost, will provide each local church with as many spiritual gifts as necessary for that church to function as a New Testament Church. Christian counselors need to rejoice because of their gifts from God. We are not alone in this world of sin and despair. God is indeed still with His people. Therefore, we are assured that our-counseling is supported by the. ministry of the Holy

Ghost. When any counselor searches to counsel in his own wisdom apart from the Spirit of God, he is in opposition towards God of all creation. He rebelliously seeks to circumvent the work of God is therefore void of all usefulness.

God has given us the scripture for a purpose. This purpose is for us to know God. He has revealed Himself to us through His Word. The Holy Ghost expects us then to see God's Word in the counseling setting. The writer of Hebrews had this to say about God's Word. Hebrews 4:12:

> For the Word of God is quick and powerful and sharper than
> any two-edged sword, piercing even to the dividing asunder
> of soul and spirit, and of the joints and marrow, and is a
> discerner of the thoughts and intents of the heart.[6]

The secular counselor depends upon his humanistic training in the larger schools. He has been taught the theories of Freud, Skinner, Rogers and countless others. The secular counselor's book shelves are filled with humanistic materials that offer no real hope. These counselors are crawling in the darkness while the Christian counselor is standing on the Solid Rock who is Jesus Christ and His Word. The Bible is not a book of theories, and perhaps, as a scheme of things thought, might work. It is a book of divine truth that came from God. Paul writes in II Timothy 3: 16-17:

> All scripture is given by inspiration of God and is profitable
> for doctrine, for reproof, for correction, for instruction
> in righteousness. That the man of God may be perfect,
> thoroughly furnished unto all good works.[7]

As we see, the perfect counseling is done through the Word of. God and the ministry of the Holy Spirit. Christian counselors need to realize this and saturate themselves in the Word of God. Their counseling skills will be improved a hundred fold.

Christian counselors need to be led by the Spirit of God. We read in the book of Luke that the Lord Jesus Christ was led by the Holy Spirit. Paul tells us in Galatians 5:18, that we are to be led by the Holy Spirit. The leading of the Holy Spirit will always be in harmony with the Holy Scripture. God's Spirit will not lead us where His written Word does not direct. Counseling cannot be effective apart from the Word of God, and God's Spirit will not lead the Christian counselor to the sacred gems of His Word. The Holy Ghost is indeed in the business of counseling and helping God's children overcome the problems and troubles of this life. We need to be aware and to utilize the Holy Spirit's help in every aspect of our lives and ministry. The scripture should be the center of any counseling.

Every type of counseling session should center on the Word of God. Counseling without the Word of God can be expected to end in failure. Many Christians counselors today are walking with the wrong partner. The works of the secular counselor must be cast aside. The Christian counselor needs to take up the Holy Word of God and go forth in the strength and power of the Holy Spirit of God.

Chapter II

Talk Therapy (Psychotherapy)

Counselors, psychologists, sociologists and other professionals agree that communication is of the upmost importance in any relationship. There is a genuine need for people to talk to one another. There are many ways in which to communicate with one another. There are more books being printed today than ever before. We live in modern society where we can communicate with the other side of the world by radio, phone, T.V., Fax, Satellite, Computers/Internet, etc. This would have been impossible only a hundred years ago. Truly we live in a modern age. Yet, with all the modern devices that we have, we still have a communication problem. We must learn to communicate with one another. Adams speaks of communication thus:

> Communication that gets across what one wants to get across
> or receives the response that one seeks is not necessarily the
> only kind of successful communication.[8]

One of the major reasons people do not communicate is the simple fact that many do not speak the truth. We have a serious credibility problem in the world today. Not only is there a credibility gap in politics (as we have seen from the Clinton presidency) and the business world but the Church of the Living God has been affected by this ungodly communication gap. There are believers in the Christian Church that are not living according to the Word of God. They seek to hide their sins in the closet. They refuse to seek counsel from God.

Hence, they have a tremendous communication problem with our Heavenly Father. This problem is not new. It has been around since the beginning of time. Adam and Eve had a communication problem with God in the Garden of Eden after their fall. Instead of seeking the face of God and sharing their guilt and shame they chose to hide themselves in the bushes. God ever seeks for His people to be open and honest with Him. President Ronald Reagan is considered by many to be the great communicator. However, the great communicator is God! God alone is ever ready to speak to His people: Isaiah the Prophet records the words of God: Isaiah 1:18:

> *Come now and let us reason together, saith the Lord: though your sins be as scarlet, they shall be as white as snow; though they are red like crimson, they shall be as wool.*[9]

God chose to relate Himself most intimately with man. He has chosen to give us His written Word, the Holy Scriptures. Not only has He chosen to communicate with us through His Word but also through His own Son, the Lord Jesus Christ. Jesus Christ, God's own eternal Son came to this earth as a human being. He was made in the flesh and walked among the sons of men. How blessed it was when Jesus, the Son of God, lived and walked among men. The words that fell from the lips of Jesus were the sweetest words ever uttered. This was communication at the highest level. Today God still speaks to us through His Word and the Holy Spirit. God has—not left-us-alone. He is still with us.

The gift of language that God has given us implies the duty of communicating His truth. Christian counselors therefore should fear no evil. They should take a back seat to no secular counselor. God has given us all that we need.

Communication does have its flaws. However, flaws are not with God. These flaws come from the heart of sinful men. Satan, the devil, was the first to pollute communication. It was Satan that cast doubt on God's Word in the Garden of Eden. Jesus Christ calls Satan for what he is: John 8:44

> *When he speaketh a lie, he speaketh of his own; for he is a liar, and father of it.*[10]

Satan then is the father of all communication which involves untruth (lies). When counselors or counselees question the Word of God be sure that Satan is standing in the background enjoying every word. Man listened to Satan's first lie and it cost him eternal fellowship with God without physical death. Satan today casts doubts, lies, etc. to hinder the people of God. When Satan speaks many of God's people turn a deaf ear to him.

After the fall of Adam, the sweet fellowship he had with God was broken. God no longer walked in the cool of the evening with Adam. Adam no longer heard those wonderful words from the lips of God. God created man to be a social creature. Man needs to communicate with others. When this communication and fellowship is not present men will suffer. Because of Adam's broken fellowship with God he began to suffer the misery of alienation, and began to show it. Adam's relationship and communication with God was not in shambles because of sin. We often wonder what would have happened if Adam had not rebelled against God. Perhaps this is an unfair question. However, one thing is for certain, his fellowship with God would not have been broken and he would never have suffered physical death.

Adam did find forgiveness from God. No doubt this forgiveness came through communication. However, the lie had entered the human race. Now man would learn to depend on half truths and human reasoning. He would become a creature of blame shifting and attempting to cover up his sin in any way. When this is done it only adds to the communication problems we have with God and our fellow man.

No it should be more than a passing interest to note, that every one of the major problems that exist today are found in germ form in the Garden of Eden. There is nothing new under the sun. Every problem that we face has been faced before by someone else. Many of the problems are in communication with God or others. For example, counselees will often suffer from a guilty conscience. It is very clear that Adam also suffered from a guilty conscience. Jacob, the patriarch of old certainly suffered from a guilty conscience (Genesis 32:1-32). Every person born into the human race is subject to communication problems, only one is excluded. Jesus of course, did not have any of the problems and sins that are common to man. He is God and thus cannot be tempted to sin. Those who teach that He could have sinned do err and do not understand the Scripture. All other members of the human race have been born with the nature of Adam. Therefore, without Christ, man is totally depraved, and subject to all manner of sin. This sinful nature causes a communication with problem with man and God. Only Christ can bridge this great gap. The capacity for self-evaluation, that God built into man now activated painful inner situations. Man now knows that there is something in,-his inner soul that tells him something is wrong. Man does not have to be a genius to know that there is no peace, joy, and happiness in his life. Man's conscience accuses him of sin. Many times when the conscience convicts and condemns, man runs in the wrong direction. The sinful nature drives him from God instead of to God.

Though sinful man may try to hide from God and escape the problems of this life it is impossible. It is utterly impossible to avoid the presence of God. The sinner may seek to hide from the face of God. However, when he turns to one side or the other, God is there. We can't escape His presence. There have been many throughout the ages that have tried to hide from God. They have tried without success. Every man, woman, boy and girl must come to terms with God in order to have peace in this life. That peace can only come through the shed blood of the Lord Jesus Christ.

When Adam came from the bushes he was naked and ashamed. Adam attempted to hide his nakedness with fig leaves. This was man's futile attempt to please God without Christ. It is interesting to note that the only thing our blessed Lord ever cursed in this life was the barren fig tree (Matthew 21:19). God wants men to come out and speak to him and seek his forgiveness. Adam further complicated matters by attempting to handle matters his own way, rather than seeking the help of God. Adam not only committed a sin he added to his troubles by trying to flee the scene. He then attempted to cover up his sin. No doubt Adam would fit very well into modern society.

The age in which we live could very well be called the great cover up period in the history of the world. The cover up act is widespread in the Christian and secular world today. Adam could not cover his sin from the eyes of God. God pressed and pointed his finger at the very center of Adam's heart. In spite of Adam's attempt to avoid his sin, God pressed the issue. God confronted non-ethically, forcing him to deal with the problem. Even under pressure of the Divine confrontation, Adam lied and did what the modern man does today, he shifted the blame. He passed the blame on to Ave. Eve in turned passed the blame on to the Serpent. Neither Adam or Eve were willing to own up to their personal responsibilities-for their sins. Instead each tried to justify themselves by laying blame at the door of the other. These sinful lies became other additional factors in the problem of communication. Adam saw the truth in this when he wrote:

> *Poor communication will lead to other problems stemming from misunderstandings, etc.*[11]

There must be communication between God and man in order to have a good relationship. When communication is broken with God or man serious problems will arise. The modern family today is faced with serious communication difficulties. Take for instance, a family in which communication has broken down. The husband and his wife have been at each other's throats from the very beginning of their marriage. Communication between the two has completely broken. The following story will help us understand the problem communication better.

George is a devout Christian. He was raised in a Christian home and attended Church regularly. However, he had a problem with his wife Susan that he hasn't been able to work out. It seems that their marriage may end up in divorce court. For an entire week he has thought of nothing else. He wants to save his marriage and have a good relationship with his wife. He goes home one night determined to solve their problems. He opens the door of his home and says to Susan we got to do something about our problems. Before he can say another word she goes on the attack. Unkind words are said that can never be recanted. Much pain and sorrow have been caused. She cries out, "If you continue to act the way you have been lately, those problems will seem very little. We are going to have it out here and now. I intend to settle this problem once and for all. This problem will be settled my way or not at all". He retreats to the living room wondering what to do. He asked, "What is the use of staying in this marriage? Perhaps the best thing to do is end this sham right now.

I am trying to resolve our problems and this woman wants to start World War III. I give up, there is nothing else I can do!"

Meanwhile God's Spirit has been dealing with the heart of Susan. She thinks about the way she talked to her husband. She goes into the living room and sits at the Knees of George. She begins, "When you came home tonight" . . . Now George is raging mad, he stares at his wife and says, "Yes, when I came in the door it all began all over again. I can't take any more of this conflict". This adds fuel to the fire and Susan storms out of the room to fume over supper, and cries, "What is the use?" She decides to end the marriage in divorce.

It is clear to see what a communication breakdown will do. Genesis 3 presents us with this first marital communication problem. Because of sin, men break communication with each other. Then sin hinders the full communication of people to continue. This may be called a complete communication breakdown. Under the very best of circumstances it is not easy to reestablish broken communication. Communications breakdown is a serious problem. The Tower of Babel presents a clear picture of what broken communication can do. Communication binds people together. It is only by communication that the problems of people can be resolved. When counselors meet with couples experiencing marital problems communication should be the Counselor's number one priority.

Counselees who are unwilling to communicate will never solve their problems. Counselors must encourage both parties to have open, honest communication with each other. Here, the counselor will face a tremendous task. Many couples or families will refuse to meet with a Counselor. However, through communication these problems can most often be solved.

Another important point of communication is that the counselee must be reconciled with himself and God. This restoration can only be done through the saving power of the Lord Jesus Christ. All communication of any purpose must be done through Christ Jesus. Communication must be administered in love. Such love exists only in the realm of God's eternal truth.

Communication can be established through the help of God. This is due to the fact of the cross of Jesus. It was God who took the initiative in bridging the gap between Him and fallen man. It was God who opened the doors of communication with sinful man. Because of the death, burial, and resurrection of Jesus Christ all communication problems between God and man can be solved. Man is also able to communicate with his fellow humans because of the work of Christ on the cross.

Communication was broken in the Garden of Eden, as has already been mentioned. God's truth was doubted, denied and scorned. Man began his downhill slide that has landed him in all sorts of problems. God demands that men communicate in an honest, open manner. Communication can be obtained through the aid of the Holy Spirit of God. Communication must be based on the truth of God.

Chapter III

The Minister-Counselor

The Bible teaches us that pastors are more than preachers. Preaching the gospel is indeed their most important function. However, this is not their only duty. They are to be Christian Counselors. They are to be able to teach the Word of God which will enable them to be Christian Counselors. They need also to be good listeners with a sincere heart to help the people who come to them for guidance. The pastor needs the wisdom of God to listen to, two or more parties who are having problems and offer them sound advice and guidance. The pastor must be in fellowship with God in order to be of any use to others.

There are times when some pastor counselors forget their place in the plan of God. They tend sometimes to assume the role of God. They tend sometimes to assume the role of God in the counseling process. Christian Counselors must remember it is God and only God who can solve the deep seated sins of man. Most secular Counselors can give no lasting solution to the problems people face. Only the Christian pastor counselor has the tools necessary to give lasting hope.

The pastor is required from the Word of God and from God directly, to meet the needs of those who might require his services. We are further told, that the man of God must be thoroughly furnished unto all good works. This certainly must include the area of counseling, for our very day in which we live demands it, our people are hungry for it and cry out loud for it. Therefore, the pastor must be learned and skilled and able to administer it without delay. I believe that just as surely as we exist and as certain as God Almighty has entrusted and charged the ministry of the Word of God to the pastor, God will hold us accountable for counseling and its ministry through the local church; if we fail to avail ourselves to it.

So far the discussion of this study has been limited to pastoral Christian counseling, as a professional in the field. What can be said of counseling directed toward non Christians? Any such counseling so directed would not only be an attempt to resolve their immediate crisis\difficulties, but a honest effort to directs lead the person to a personal faith in the Lord Jesus Christ. Counseling is some sense a redemptive act, an attempt to reunite broken and torn pieces of lives. It is a mending process. What God has done for sinful man in and through Christ our Lord, conditioning the work the counselor performs. Counseling should follow and reflect God's order in redemption: Grace, then faith, the Gospel, then sanctification. Again, counseling must be redemptive. The way Paul proceeded in the Book of Romans, gives clear directions. He showed all people of various nationalities, cultural backgrounds, lifestyles and habits, that all have sinned. Next Paul refuted any and all false ideas of redemption through attempts to keeping the laws (for none of us are able to keep the whole law perfectly), he established the truth of justification by faith alone. Finally, he exhorted us to personal holiness through the righteousness of our Lord Jesus Christ.

Chapter IV

The Necessity for Prayer in Counseling

We are come to one of the most important aspects of Christian Counseling. Prayer is the most powerful force on the face of this earth next the Person of the Holy Spirit. Certainly all Christians know the importance of talking to God in prayer. In counseling with counselees the Counselor must depend upon prayer and the ministry of the Holy Spirit of God. Jay Adams has this to say concerning prayer:

> Power and purifying presence of the Holy Spirit must be invoked by the human Counselor as he acknowledges his own sins and inabilities.[12]

The Christian Counselor should bath himself in prayer before any counseling session. For the counselor to enter the counseling session without having been in prayer is like a soldier going into battle without his weapon. Each Counselor will have ample information of counselees to prepare for prayer. This information will have been obtained from his data file and other resources. Each counseling session will be much more constructive when it has been prayed for. God will honor those who pray and seek His face. The answers to difficult problems will come faster when we pray and seek the guidance of God. James the brother of our Lord wrote: James 5:16:

Confess your faults one to another, and pray one for another
that ye may be healed. The effectual fervent prayer of a
righteous man availeth much.[13]

There are those who laugh at Counselors who spend time in prayer. If these secular Counselors would take the time to compare their rate of success with that of Christian counselors they would not be so quick to laugh. Prayer is indeed the most important element in the counseling process.

Prayer should always end the counseling session. It would be good to begin the counseling session with prayer in the presence of the counselees. Most all people, saved or lost appreciate someone praying for them. With prayer counselees come to know that the Counselor really cares about his or her problem. They will even be times when prayer is called for during the counseling session. There is certainly nothing wrong with this. The counselee himself may even want to pray. The Word of God does bring conviction on people. When God convicts people of sin or whatever do not stand in His way. Counselors need to stand back at times and let the Holy Spirit do His work. He is far better at the work of counseling than any sinful human being.

The Christian Counselor should never pressure the counselee into praying. This the work of the Holy Spirit. Many counselees are turned off by this and may not return for the next session. There is much truth to the old proverb which says: "You can lead a mule to the water trough but you can't make him drink." The Christian Counselor must use much wisdom in this matter.

Prayer at the end of the session by the Counselor is very important. This time could be the most important in the life of the counselee. The prayer could focus in on the content of the counseling session. If there was success the prayer could be directed to praising God for the success. If closed doors had been opened, thank God for it.

There may be times when the counselee should not pray. There are Scriptures that teach that our prayers can be hindered. For example if a husband is not treating his wife right his prayers will be hindered (I Peter 3:7). Prayer must be done in the right spirit and attitude. If the counselee is angry or upset prayer may not the thing to do at the time. Jay Adams suggests when counselees are not in the right frame of mind for prayer something may still be done. He writes:

> Prayer may be suggested as homework. Not only should regular prayer be advised for all counselees, but prayer may be prescribed specifically as a solution to a problem.[14]

The Christian Counselor that does not use prayer in the counseling session is wasting a valuable resource. God hears the prayers of his people when they come in faith and truth. There is great power in prayer. Minirth describes prayer thus:

> Through prayer we can incorporate supernatural strength. Through prayer we can call upon supernatural powers to help us in our depression.[15]

Chapter V

God's Requirements for a Good Marriage

Today marriage is a very unstable institution. The divorce rate is higher than it has ever been. Families are breaking up at an alarming rate. Some homes today could be described as a war zone. Fighting and name calling are the common thing. The children of these families are the great losers.

What is the problem? Why are families in such disarray today? The answer is easy to find. God is not in the center of the family. For any family to be truly happy Jesus Christ must be the Lord of the home.

The Bible has much to say about spirit-filled marriages. Ephesians 5: 22-33; 6:1-4 gives the guidelines for a successful marriage.

Wives submit yourselves unto your own husbands, as unto the Lord. For the husband is the head of the wife, even as Christ is the head of the Church; and He is the Savior of the body. Therefore, as the Church is subject unto Christ, so let the wives be to their own husbands in everything. Husbands, love your wives, even as Christ also loved the Church, and gave himself for it, that He might sanctify and cleanse it with the washing of water by the Word; that he might present it to himself a glorious church, not having spot, or wrinkle, or any such thing; but that it should be holy and without blemish. So ought men to love their wives as their own bodies. He that loveth his wife loveth himself. For no man ever hate his flesh, but nouriseth and cherisheth it, even as the Lord the Church; for we are members of his body, of His flesh, and of His bones. For this cause shall a man leave his father and mother, and shall be joined unto his wife, and they shall be one flesh. This is a great mystery, but I speak concerning the Church.

Nevertheless, let every one of you in particular so love his wife even as himself; and the wife, see that she reverance her husband. Children, obey your parents in the Lord; for this is right. Honor thy father and mother (which is the first commandment with promise), that it may be well with thee, and thou mayest live long on the earth. And ye fathers, provoke not your children to wrath, but bring them up in the nurture and admonition of the Lord.[16]

The first guideline for a successful marriage is for the husband to assume the role as head of the house (vs. 22-23). Many modern liberal thinkers today believe this is old fashioned and out of date. The Word of God changes not. If they want to have a successful marriage you will have to follow the instructions of God, Paul writes that wives are to submit themselves to their own husbands (vs. 22). The husband is the head of the wife, even as Christ is the head of the Church. When husbands and wives reverse roles only sorrow can follow. Many family problems today exist because wives assume the role as head of the family. God is not pleased with husbands who sit back and refuse to accept their God given responsibility.

The second guideline is for husbands to love their wives (vs. 25). Many husbands treat their wives like a worn out shoe. God expects husbands to love, honor, and cherish their wives. Paul goes to great length to emphasize this. The Holy Spirit of God is well aware of the shortcomings of many men in this area.

The third guideline involves the obedience of children (vs. 6:1-3). Paul reminds children of the fifth commandment (6:2). children are to honor their parents all the days of their lives. If this is done God promises a special blessing (a long life upon the earth). Many children today have broken this commandment of God. Some children refuse to heed the advice of parents. Many resent their parents. This type of attitude can never please God.

A fourth guideline is found in Ephesians 6:4. This is one commandment that is often overlooked. Parents are not to provoke their children to wrath, but bring them up in the nurture and admonition of the Lord. The word provoke means to stir up to anger. When parents do this they do not only sin against their children but also against God. We hear stories everyday how some parents go off the deep end and abuse their children. Many of these parents are well respected members of the community. Marriage and family life is the most sacred human institution on the face of this earth. Paul likens it to the love of God for His Church. Jesus Christ died and gave Himself for His Church (5:25). He has sanctified and cleansed the Church (5:26). There will come a great day when Christ will present the Church to Himself without spot or wrinkle. This is what our blessed Lord Jesus thinks of the family. We have guidelines for a happy and full home life if only we heed His Word.

Chapter VI

The Impact of Separation, Divorce and Remarriage

A new statistic came out not long ago that said one in every two marriages end in divorce. This is no surprise. When people turn away from God and seek the temporary pleasures of sin the family is sure affected.

The Bible teaches much about marriage and divorce. Our Lord Jesus said: Matthew 19:5-6:

> For this cause shall a man leave his father and mother, and shall cleave to his wife, and they two shall be one flesh? Wherefore, they are no more two, but one flesh. What therefore, God hath joined together, let no man put asunder.[17]

These verses clearly teach that God hates divorce. God clearly states that when two people are joined together in marriage that no one is to break up the marriage. Jesus Christ further states that in Matthew 19:9:

> Whoever shall put away his wife, except it be for fornication, and shall marry another committeth adultery; and whosoever marrieth-her who is put away doth commit adultery.[18]

Many people today including Christians try to sidestep the teachings of our Lord. We can never please God when we attempt to do this. God intends for marriage to be for life. Many unsaved people believe that God's law concerning marriage only apply to Christians. This is not true. All men saved or lost are responsible to the laws of God.

Yes, Jesus Christ did permit divorce on the grounds of fornication. If one partner of a marriage is unfaithful the other has the God given right of divorce. Sexual sins in a marriage are extremely repugnant to God. The marriage partners are to be holy and pure to each other. Paul speaks of the purity of marriage in: I Corinthians 6: 15-18.

> *Know ye not your bodies are the members of Christ? Shall I, then, take the members of Christ, and make them members of an harlot? God forbid. What? Know ye not that he who is joined to an harlot is one body? For two saith he, shall be one flesh. But he that is joined unto the Lord is one spirit. Flee fornication. Every sin that a man doeth is outside the body; but he that committeth, fornication sinneth against his own body.[19]*

It is most important to remember that Jesus only permits divorce where fornication is involved. He does not command it! Forgiveness and reconciliation should always be the goal of troubled marriages. When fornication occurs in a-marriage the offended partner should not run to busybodies, lawyers, or judges. The offended partner should seek the face of God. Only God can heal broken hearts. He alone can heal the hurt and pain that comes to the betrayed partner. God alone can deal with the heart of the sinning partner to bring conviction and repentance. Many marriages could be saved if people would only seek the help of Jesus Christ. Instead of leaning on so called experts the offended partner should read the Word of God. The offended partner should seek God's guidance and leadership through the Scripture.

The greatest losers of any divorce are the children. Parents have a tremendous responsibility in raising their children in the nurture and admonition of the Lord. We often wonder how any man or woman could walk away from their children. How can people destroy a marriage and cause such pain and sorrow to the children they profess to love. The answer is sin. Sin blinds the hearts and minds of people. When someone is thinking of divorce they should stop and seek the guidance of Jesus Christ. Troubled couples should stop and seek the guidance of Jesus Christ. Anyone considering divorce should stop and consider the awful pain involved. Troubled couples need to open the Word of God and seek the advice and counsel of God. Any pastor that has been called to God to preach His Word will be glad to sit down and share the Scripture and pray for troubled souls. Divorce is not the answer.

First Corinthians chapter seven is the great chapter that deals with marriage. The Scripture clearly teaches that God has ordained marriage. It is a most holy institution that was blessed by our Savior at the wedding of Cana. John 2: 1,2.

> *And the third day there was a marriage in Cana, of Galilee;*
> *and the mother of Jesus was there. And both Jesus was called,*
> *and His disciples, to the marriage.*[20]

Many marriages today are ending up in divorce court. Couples with marital problems are bombarded with bad advice from all directions. Some lawyers advertise their services as $100 dollars to handle a divorce case. A miserable fee to end a marriage that ordained for life.

Troubled couples need to seek help from God. The Bible gives us God's answers to all our problems. We hear every day of husbands or wives who abandon the other. Many wives leave their husbands or else have him barred from the home. What does God have to say about all of this? His counsel is what man needs! God clearly states in verse ten that the wife should not leave her husband. Verse eleven states that the husband should not leave his wife. Divorce is clearly a sin against God.

Divorce is sin and we live in a sinful world. God foresaw how sinful men would live and act. God knew that multitudes of marriages would end in divorce. Marriages end in divorce because of sin. When divorce happens God commands that the partners should remain unmarried. I Corinthians 7:11

But if she depart, let her remain unmarried, or be reconciled to
her husband; and let not the husband put away his wife.[21]

However, if one of the partners were guilty of fornication the
other has the God given to remarry: Matthew 19:9.

And I say unto you whosoever shall put away his wife, except
it be for fornication, and shall marry another, committeth
adultery, and whosoever marrieth her who is put away doth
commit adultery.[22]

Even then forgiveness and reconciliation should be the goal. The
sinning partner should repent and seek the forgiveness of God and
his\her spouse.

Paul now deals with the question of mixed marriages (saved and
lost partners). Should the believer put away the lost partner? If the
lost partner wants to continue the marriage the believing partner is
obligated to remain. Many people seek divorce on the grounds of an
unbelieving partner. This is clearly not what the Word of God teaches.
God has a special reason for the believing partner to remain in a
marriage. I Corinthians 7:14.

For the unbelieving husband is sanctified by the wife, and the
unbelieving wife is sanctified by the husband; else were your
children unclean, but now are they holy.[23]

The unbelieving partner is sanctified by the believer. This does
not mean that they are saved by the believer. The Bible teaches
that al men must answer to God for their own sins. The word sanctify
means to "set apart." All believers have been sanctified (set apart)
by God. Here unbelievers are said to be sanctified (set apart) by the
believing spouse. This is a principle that is found throughout the Bible.
Many times lost people are blessed because of their relationship
with saved people. Carnal believers such as Lot was blessed because
of his closeness to Abraham. Genesis 13: 1-8.

And Abram went up out of Egypt, he, and his wife, and all
that he had. Lot with him, into the Negev. And Abram was

very rich in cattle, in silver, and in gold. And he went on his journeys from the Negev even to Bethel, unto the place where his tent had been at the beginning, between Bethel and Hai; Unto the place of the altar, which he had made there at the first: and there Abram called on the name of the Lord. And Lot also, who went with Abram, had flocks, and herds, and tents. And the land was not able to bear them, that they might dwell together; for their substance was great, so that they could not dwell together. And there was strife between the herdsmen of Abram's cattle and the herdsmen of Lot's cattle; and the Canaanite and the Perizzite dwelt then in the land. And Abram said unto Lot. Let there be no strife, I pray thee, between me and thee, and between my herdsmen and thy herdsmen; for we are brethren.[24]

The Holy Spirit of God seeks to bring conviction on the unbelieving partner. The Holy Spirit also seeks to bless the children in a special way. Malachi 2: 14, 15

Yet ye say, (Why)? Because the Lord hath witness between thee and the wife of thy youth, against whom thou hast dealt treacherously; yet is she thy companion, and the wife of thy covenant. And did not he make one? Yet had he the residue of the spirit. And (why) one? That he might seek a godly seed. Therefore, take heed to your spirit and let none deal treacherously against the wife of his youth.[25]

What if the unbelieving partner abandons their spouse? Is the believing partner then free to remarry? God says that a partner is no longer under bondage when they are abandoned. I Corinthians 7:15

But if the unbelieving depart, let then depart. A brother or a sister is not under bondage in such cases; but God hath called us to peace.[26]

The believing spouse that has been deserted is free to remarry and put their lives back together and live for the glory of God.

Jay Adams offers an interesting solution for an abandon spouse where both partners profess to be Christians. He treats the subject at length. His Presbyterian Reformed theology is evident in his treatment. He writes thus:

The problem remains, however, as to what must be done when two professing Christians fail to keep their marriage together and reconciliation does not take place. Let us say that a husband who is a professing Christian refuses to be reconciled to his wife. Perhaps he has even left her. Reconciliation has been attempted by the wife. If she continues to insist upon reconciliation (according to Matthew 18), but fails in her attempts at private confrontation, she must.-take one or two others from the church and confront her husband. Suppose she does that and he refuses to hear them. In that case she is required to submit the problem officially to the church, which ultimately may be forced, by his adamant refusal to be reconciled, to excommunicate him for contumacy. Excommunication, Christ says changes his status to that of a heathen and a publican, i.e., someone outside of the church (Matthew 18:17). Now he must be treated as a heathen and a publican. That means, for instance, that after reasonable attempts to reconcile him to the church and his wife, he must taken to court (I Corinthians 6: 1-8) forbids brethren to go to law against one another or to sue for a divorce (only, of course, if the excommunicated one deserts his partner).

By following the reconciliation dynamic, hopefully there will be reconciliation in most cases. Whenever the principles of biblical reconciliation are followed faithfully, discipline rarely reaches the highest level of excommunication. Most marriages not only can be saved, but by proper help may be changed radically for good. But in those few cases where reconciliation is refused, the believer who seeks it is not left in a state of limbo. He has a course of action to pursue, and if it leads to excommunication and desertion he is no longer obligated to remain married indefinitely. This is true only if the believer's marriage partner during the whole process of discipline has failed to demonstrate evidence of repentance and faith, if that partner has been excommunicated, and if he (or she) wishes to dissolve the marriage. Continued rejection of the help an authority of Christ and His church finally leads to excommunication.

An excommunicated party who continues to be unrepentant must be looked upon and treated as a heathen and publican. He shows no signs of a work of grace. When he has been put outside of the church and still evidences of salvation, the believing partner may deal with him as with an unbeliever. This means that if he leaves the believer under these circumstances, the latter is no longer under "bondage." The word in I Corinthians 7: 21 governing the relationship of a believer to an unbelieving marriage partner then comes into effect. By plugging in the reconciliations discipline dynamic to the marriage-divorce-remarriage problem, the solution to ninety-nine percent of these cases that heretofore may have seemed unsolvable immediately may be seen. Most parties hopefully will come to reconciliation, but those who will not repent and be reconciled should be disciplined. Either way, matters are not left at loose ends.[27]

Chapter VII

Fornication

Today we live in a sexual revolution. Single people today are bombarded by sexual pressures of all kind. Sex before marriage is accepted by many as the common thing. The society in which we live seems to be obsessed with sex. The television screen is filled with sexual programs. The movie theaters are showing more sexual films then ever before. It seems that the American public is crying out for more and more. Sex was intended by God to be for marriage. Now it is considered out of date and old fashioned not to have premarital sex. Premarital sex is a moral sickness that has swept across this land.

The Bible has much to say about premarital sex. God refers to premarital sex as fornication. Fornication is clearly condemned in the Word of God. Premarital sex distorts God's plan for sexual relationships between men and women. Gary Collins describes as:

> Unhealthy sexuality distorts God's perfect plan for human beings. It destroys intimacy and communication, is self-centered, and often expresses a desire to manipulate, control, or hurt another person. The experience is pleasurable; it dulls one's sense of loneliness, and it gives a feeling of intimacy, but all of this is temporary, dehumanizing, and ultimately unfulfilling.[28]

Premarital sex certainly poses many problems. This is why God so strongly condemns it in His Word. Since premarital sex is not God's plan for the human race it is therefore sinful. It should be noted that fornication in the Bible refers to premarital sex whereas adultery refers to someone having sexual relations with someone other than one's spouse. Adultery as well as fornication is condemned by God.

There are some today who might consider sex sinful it its self. This is not true. Sex was created by God. When God created Adam and Eve He made them sexual beings, he made both different so that they could enjoy sexual intimacy including sexual intercourse. Jay Adams writes concerning sex:

> Sexual relations within marriage are holy and good. God encourages relations and warns against their cessation.[29]

With the fall of Adam all manner of sin came to the human race. Sex also became distorted and blemished by the sinful practices of man. Paul writes concerning fornication: I Corinthians 6: 13-18.

> Meats for the belly, and the belly for meats; but God shall destroy both it and them. Now the body is not for fornication, but for the Lord; and the Lord for the body. Flee fornication. Every sin that a man doeth is outside the body; but he that committeth fornication sinneth against his own body.[30]

God in His Word continues to warn men of sin of fornication. Many modern young couples fall into this sin. They say they are love and want to please their partner. They argue that they are planning to get married. Therefore, there seems to be nothing wrong with premarital sex. This is completely the opposite of what God says in His Word. If two young people are in love and cannot reframe themselves from sin, then they need to heed the advice of God. I Corinthians 7:9.

> But if they cannot have self-control, let them marry: for it is better to marry than to burn.[31]

There are many reasons why people commit fornication. I realize that many people would like to drop the word fornication and simply use the term premarital sex. The word fornication carries and odor of sinfulness with it. Those who get caught up in this word game seem to be experiencing guilt and shame associated with fornication. Through inclusive some of the following are major causes for premarital sex.

1. The world around us. The society in which we live stimulates people to sexual behavior, Much of the clothing today invites sexual arousal. The movies, television, and magazines play upon the human appetite for sex. Pornography also has clearly played a large role in the increase of premarital sex. Peer pressure is very intense upon young people. Adolescents are tempted on every turn to participate in premarital sex. Many young people are lonely and feel deserted by parents. These young people need the love and affection the same as adults. When this is missing they ultimately will turn to each other for sexual gratification.

2. Sin Traps. This involves motels, hotels, apartments, etc. We live in a very open and convenient society. America today is a mobile nation. It is no problem to get to motels or other places to meet people. Birth control has also played a large role in fornication. Women no longer need to fear an unwanted pregnancy.

3. Low morals. There are many who would object to this term. The teachings of the Holy Scripture are not longer considered of value to many. Premarital sex is no longer considered sin by a large part of today's population. Premarital sex is widely discussed and widely accepted as the modern way of living. School children in the very grades of school are being taught sex education. Marriage is no longer considered a sacred institution. Couples find living together has less responsibilities. Divorced people no longer reframe from sexual intercourse.

4. Curiosity. This may well be the number one cause of fornication among young people. Many unmarried people hear the thrills of sex and conclude that the world is leaving them behind. They therefore, attempt to catch up as fast as they can.

5. A feeling of inferiority. Many people realize that the sexual revolution is passing them by. This creates within them a feeling of insecurity and loneliness. They began to feel that they have no real purpose in life. In order to be in the in crowd they turn to thrills of cheap sex, hoping for some kind of enjoyment. Most often they find that cheap sex only leads to more loneliness and pain.

6. The need for love. Man is a creature that needs the companionship of others. Man was thus created and designed to be by his Maker. The Word of God reads: Genesis 2: 18.

   And the Lord God said, it is not good that the man should be alone; I will make him an help meet for him.[32]

When people are alone and lonely they are going against their God given nature. They will often turn to premarital sex as a result.

7. Rebellion against parents. Many young people tend to rebel against parents. This is nothing new. The Bible tells of Absalom's rebellion even led to his fornication with David's concubines. II Samuel 16: 21-22.

   And Ahitophel said unto Absalom, Go in unto thy father's concubines, whom he hath left to keep the house, and all Israel shall hear that thou abhorred of thy father; then shall the hands of all that are with thee be strong. So they spread Absalom a tent upon the top of the house; and Absalom went in unto his father's concubines in the sight of all Israel.[33]

8. The Devil. It is true that Satan gets more credit than he deserves. Man has always been quick to blame his sins on someone else. The Devil is not to blame for all the problems of this world. However, he is our great enemy. The Scripture describes our battle thus: Ephesians 6: 12.

   For we wrestle not against flesh and blood, but against powers, against the rulers of the darkness of this world, against spiritual wickedness in high places.[34]

As stated above we live in a time of great sexual temptation. Fornication and other sexual sins are constantly before our eyes. Satan uses this perversion of sex to entice many to sin. Even God's own children often fall into the snare of Satan. Sin always produces terrible side effects. Premarital sex has many side effects that create untold problems for its participants. All sin that has not been confessed to God must be judged. The Bible teaches that God will forgive all manner of sin. John the Apostle writes: I John 1:9.

If we confess our sins, He is faithful and just to forgive us our sins, and to cleanse us from all unrighteousness.[35]

Untold multitudes of people today continue in their sin and refuse to heed the advice of God. God stands ready to receive sinners into His open arms and forgive them of their sins if they will only repent and go to Him.

Insensitively toward fornication does not always lead to guilt and repentance. Research has found that few people involved in premarital sex feel any guilt or remorse. Gary Collins states that:

> A perusal of the research in this area indicates that little or no guilt following nonmarital sex, especially if the participants feel a genuine affection for each other. And as sex apart from marriage continues, initial qualms and insecurities often disappear, at least temporarily.[36]

People's insensitivity toward premarital sex does not make it right in the eyes of God. As stated above it is possible for even Christians to fall into the sin of fornication. They do this against the will of the Holy Spirit of God. Lost people will commit fornication and never bat an eye. One Christian lady told me that at one time in her life before she was saved that she would leave her Husband at home, she would then go and meet men at different places. It made no matter who they were. She said she would hop into bed with anyone. God convicted her of this sin and now she is a fine Christian lady serving her Lord and Savior. The Bible teaches that God's Spirit will not always deal in such a way with the heart of sinful men. Paul writes in the Book of Romans. Romans 1: 24, 27-29.

Wherefore, God gave them up to uncleanness, through the lusts of their own hearts, to dishonor their own bodies between themselves: And likewise also men, leaving the natural use of the woman, burned in their lust one toward another; men working with men that which is unseemly, and receiving in themselves that recompense of their error which was meet. And even as they did not like to retain God in their knowledge, God gave them over to a reprobate mind, to do those things which are not convenient, being filled with all unrighteousness, fornication, wickedness, covetousness, maliciousness, full of envy, murder, debate, deceit, malignity, whisperers.[37]

Many today like to think of God as only a loving Being. However, God is also a God of judgment. When men refuse to repent they must face the judgment of God. These verses teach that there is a point in a person's life where God's Spirit no longer deals with him. That is why it is so important to obey the Spirit of God when He brings conviction on the heart. Most all believe that premarital sex leaves an ugly scar. These scars can show up in the following ways:

1. Emotional confusion. The mind is an unusual part of the body. Emotional turmoil can reap havoc on a person. People who participate in premarital sex often experience fear, anger, depression, guilt, anxiety, low self-esteem and so forth. These are feelings the human soul can do without. It is clear to everyone that the young people involved in premarital sex today are going through a psychological struggle.
2. Weak relationships. People who are involved in premarital sex seem to have a poor relationship with other people. Many married couples who participated in premarital sex find it hard to completely trust their partners in marriage. In ray counseling ministry I have discovered that people who took part in premarital sex was much more likely to have an affair after marriage. This is true with men and women.
3. Spiritual weakness. Christians can't sin against God and live in peace. God simply will not let this happen. When a person is saved the Holy Spirit of God comes and indwells his body.

For those who don't accept this truth need to read the Word of God. Romans 8: 9.

But ye are not in the flesh, but in the Spirit, if so be that the Spirit of God dwell in you. How if any man have not the Spirit of Christ, he is none of his.[38]

4. Physical problems. Since 1973 over twenty million unborn babies have been murdered. Abortion is the great sin among many people today. Most abortions would not be if people would stop the practice of premarital sex. We also have venereal disease as the result of premarital sex. Not only is there venereal disease, but we are now faced with the worst disease of all, aids. Many Christians today are saying that aids is a judgment from God upon sin. I will have to agree with this statement.

The pastor should not be asleep or surprised. As long as people are on this earth they are going to commit sin. The Christian Counselor needs to be ready to offer help; counseling and support. People down in the depths of sin need the help of God. God expects His people to give these folks a helping hand. There are a lot of shipwrecks on the sea of life. Somebody needs to pick up the pieces. God has chosen for his people to help in this important task.

In counseling with sinful people some forget that all have sinned. There is none of us perfect. This must be remembered when the fornicator and other sinners walk through our doors. A compassionate understanding Counselor can do a great deal of good to a person struggling in sin. The Christian Counselor must cast aside his self-righteous attitude and put on the mind of Christ. If he fails to do this he is no good to himself or anyone else.

When the Christian Counselor is confronted with premarital sex he needs to listen to the heart cries of the participants. Gary Collins writes:

Listen with sensitivity. This is a basic starting point for all counseling but sometimes it is forgotten when we are presented with sexual issues. By listening, we convey our desire to understand and our willingness to-help with the counselee's real problem.[39]

As the Counselor listens to the sexual sins of the counselee he may be shocked out of his mind. Sin is all around us. The Christian Counselor must be prepared to face the realities of life. By the grace and mercy of God he will be able to help those who come to him for counsel.

Chapter VIII

The Genesis of Human Experience

Now would be a good time to pause and consider the origin of sin. Sin like everything else had a beginning. Genesis chapter three records this terrible time of human history. The words which introduce this chapter are ominous. We are introduced to the great adversary of God and man. His person and history are not revealed here. The last book of the Bible speaks of him as the great dragon, that old serpent, called the Devil and Satan, (Rev. 12:9). Our Lord called him the murderer from the beginning, and the father of lies, (John 8:44). The word "Serpent" is the Hebrew "Nachash," which means "a shining one." This creature Satan possessed and used was of great attraction to the woman.

The Serpent created doubts in Eve's mind about God and His Word. He suggests that perhaps God was not being completely fair with Adam and Eve, despite the fact that He had granted them access to the garden. Then Satan acts as the accuser of God and uttered his lie, which, as the father of lies he still continues, "Ye shall not surely die." The steps to Eve's tragic fall are instructive, and they provide a grim warning to all who would take just the first one. She listened to Satan, then responded to him, and finally yielded by participating in sin. What choice did Eve really have? James the Apostle would have said: James 4: 7.

> Submit yourselves, therefore, to God. Resist the devil, and he will flee from you.[40]

She sought no counsel from her husband or God. She made her decision on the basis of her own judgment and reasoning.

When Adam and Eve ate the fruit, their eyes were opened. They discovered their nakedness and made themselves cloths from fig leaves. Man attempts by labor of his hands, by his religious profession and morality to cover his nakedness.

God spoke to Adam and Eve in tender mercy. These two that had been created by the hand of God had now sinned. The judgment of God came upon them and the Serpent. The earth itself was cursed on account of Adam's sin. Adam and Eve would die physically and return to the dust of the ground for their sin. The result of this tragic sin are still with us today. God was not finished with man. This fallen creature would be redeemed. Satan's attempt to ruin man eternally would fail. God had a wonderful plan. The first great prophecy of the Bible is recorded in Genesis 3: 15.

> And I will put enmity between thee and the woman, and between thy seed and her seed; he shall bruise thy head, and thou shalt bruise his heel.[41]

The prophecy of Genesis 3: 15 announces the Seed of the woman, The Lord Jesus Christ and His triumphant work over the Serpent and his work as well as the death of the Seed. Out of this prediction all prophecy is developed.

Adam and Eve were driven out of the garden so as to avoid the possibility of taking of the tree of life and living forever in a state of sin. Man should never forget that Satan is the great enemy. Satan came to Eve in the body of a serpent. The serpent may have been the most beautiful of creatures. It is evident that Satan had been eavesdropping on God and Adam. In Genesis 3:1 Satan raises the question: Genesis 3: l.

> Now the serpent was more subtle than any beast of the field which the Lord God had made. And he said unto the woman. Yea, hath God said, Ye5shall not eat of every tree of the garden?[42]

Not only is Satan a liar, but he is forever seeking to trouble the people of God.

Eve is deceived of the devil and eats of the forbidden fruit. She gives unto her husband Adam and he also partakes of the fruit. Whereas, Eve was deceived by the devil, Adam chose deliberately disobey the Word of God. When both had eaten their eyes were opened and they knew they were naked. For the first time in their lives they felt the sting of sin. The Spirit of God within them convicted them of their sin. They tried to cover their nakedness and sin with fig leaves. Instead of going before a holy merciful God with repentant hearts they depended on their own selves, and shut God out, and hid in the bushes. The covering they used to cover their bodies is most interesting. Verse seven tells us that they sewed fig leaves together. Luke tells us that the only thing Jesus ever cursed in his earthly ministry was a fig tree with no figs. Matthew 21:19.

> And when he saw a fig tree along the way, he came to it, and found nothing on it but leaves only, and said unto it, let no fruit grow on thee henceforward forever. And presently the fig tree withered away.[43]

The reason for the curse was not that there were no figs. The reason for the curse goes back to Genesis 3:7. Man's first attempt to cover his sins was with fig leaves. Only the blood of Jesus Christ can wash away man's sin.

God did not leave Adam alone to hide in sin. He came down and spoke to him in the cool of the day. It was not Adam that sought out God after the tragic sin. Adam tried to hide and cover his sin. It was God who came looking for Adam, and so it has always been. It is God who comes to seek and to save those who are lost.

Genesis 3: 10 is a tremendous testimony to the ugly nature of sin and its results. Adam heard the voice of God and was afraid. Sin destroys and separates the sinner from God, it makes him afraid. Man created in the image of God is not to hide and wallow in sin. He is to come to the throne of grace and find rest for his troubled soul.

When God questioned Adam and Eve they both answered in the way of the natural man. Each tried to put the blame on someone else. The sinner does not like to know of his lost condition.

God also pronounced judgment upon the serpent. He would be cursed above all the beasts of the earth. As stated above God also promised the coming of Jesus Christ. At the death and resurrection, He crushed the head of Satan. Judgment was also pronounced upon the woman. Her sorrow would be in childbirth. She would be in subjection to her husband.

God also pronounced judgment upon the man. The ground Adam tilled would be cursed from that day forward. Until now Adam had been keeper of the garden, he would now be the tiller of the ground. The ground would yield her fruit easy. It would be a struggle for Adam and his descendants.

God made provision for Adam. Adam attempted to cover himself with fig leaves. Fig leaves cannot cover sin, only the blood of Jesus Christ can do that! God slew an animal and made coats of skin for him. This had its fulfillment in the sacrifice of our Lord Jesus Christ. It is only the blood of Jesus that can make us right in the eyes of a Holy and righteous God.

Adam's expulsion from the garden is recorded in Genesis 3:22-24. Man now knew the difference between good and evil. Adam was driven from the Garden of Eden lest he eat of the tree of life and live forever. If Adam had eaten of this tree man would never have died. The earth would be populated with a race of sinners to live eternally in the regenerate state. Can you imagine what this world would be like if God had not driven Adam from the garden.

Friend this is not the end of the garden. For in Revelation 22 we find another garden. The tree of life is again set before man. This time man is not driven away, but he is invited to come and partake of its fruit. The river of life is also there, clear as crystal, flowing out of the throne of God and of the Lamb. The earth was cursed at Adam's fall, now there is no more curse. The most wonderful thing about this garden is that God will be there and we shall see His face.

Chapter IX

At Home in a World Full of Sins

The Christian Counselor must realize that he will meet all kinds of people. This world is filled with sin. Sin has marred the human race in extraordinary way. The Christian counselor must be prepared for those he ministers to. In order to do that he must have biblical knowledge of what sin is and how it effects man. The sins of our nation today are similar to those committed by Israel in the Bible.

We read in Hosea chapter four of the moral condition of the nation of Israel. These people had turned away from God who had so wonderfully blessed them.

Our nation today is traveling down the same path as Israel of old. We to, like Israel will reap what we sow. Someone once said that if God did not judge America He would have to apologize to Sodom and Gomorrah. God is judging America. Consider the drought 1 Crops are drying up in the fields for lack of water. God is warning this nation to turn back to Him. Will we listen to Him and repent of our sins? Will we as a nation return to God who has made us the greatest nation on the face of this earth.

There are those who say our nation is not doing so badly. They claim that we are a modern people, that we have outgrown the teachings of the Bible. Some have the idea that God smiles on the modern humanist movement of our nation. God hated sin in the days of Hosea and He hates sin today. God hates sin in spite of what the liberal humanist professes.

Compare the sins of our nation with those of Israel in the days of Hosea. In Hosea's days the people were swearing, lying, killing, stealing, and committing adultery. Those people had no knowledge of God.

No one can deny that our nation is not doing those same sins. In fact we have advanced sin to all forms of ungodly wickedness. Drug abuse is sweeping our land. Drug dealers are destroying people's lives. They even sell their poison to our children and have no shame.

Morality is this nation has hit an all time low. Adultery, fornication, pornography, and other vices seem to be the in thing with many people. We read of greed and scandal of our leaders almost every day. Many leaders have sold their soul for get rich quick schemes. People in our armed forces have sold top military secrets for sex.

Our school children are no longer allowed to pray to God in the public classroom. It is ironic that education in this nation was begun by the Church. The Church has always been the leader in the education of the people. Now the Church is considered obsolete and old fashioned. The State now considers itself to be the authority on education. The greatest irony of all is that public education was begun to teach the people to read the Bible! Now the Bible has been banned from the classroom.

Abortion is the ugliest most wicked sin of all. Over twenty million unborn babies have been murdered since 1973. These precious children have not lived to see the light of day. How long will our people stand for this mass murder of unborn children. How long will God tolerate this wicked crime before He brings this nation to its knees.

If this is not enough we now have those blasphemous, filthy, sacrilegious movie about our Blessed Savior entitled, "The Last Temptation of Christ." Jesus is seen as being shaky in the head. He is portrayed as having sex with Mary Magdalene. The movie shows Him not dying on the cross but living to an old age, this movie is a complete distortion of the life and work of our Blessed Savior.

Christians how long are we going to tolerate this sin and filth. God expects us to be about our Father's business. God expects us to cry out against sin. We need to ask God to give us the courage and boldness to speak out against the ungodly wickedness in our land.

The Old Testament book of Jeremiah echoes much of the same as Hosea. The theme of Jeremiah's message is as relevant today as it was when it was first uttered to the Jewish people centuries ago. The people of God wandered far away from Him. The nation was sinking deeper and deeper into sin. Our nation today is in the same situation! Multitudes of people today are living in the depths of sin. Satan has blinded their eyes from the truth, In spite of all this sin is God is willing to forgive. Our Lord promised that those who come to Him would be saved. Christian Counselors must never forget this.

Jeremiah was a faithful servant of God. Jeremiah felt pain as perhaps no other prophet did. His life was one of suffering and misery. Only the grace of God kept Jeremiah going. The book is filled with instances where the prophet's faith and confidence in God are shown.

Jeremiah was a faithful preacher of the Word of God. His message was hard. The people rejected the prophet and his message. Not only did they reject his message, they attempted to destroy the prophet. The great grandchildren of these Jewish people would one day treat the Savior of the world in much the same way. Christian pastors today may expect more of the same.

The sermons of Jeremiah pricked the hearts of the people. However, this only made their hatred of him even greater. Jeremiah did not water down his message as many are doing today. The prophet spoke out against the idolatry of the people with a boldness that can only come from God. Someone once said that immortality and idolatry are always found together. This was the case in the days of Jeremiah. This was a time of great moral decay. People from all walks of Jewish life lived in sin. The common people and the priests along with the elders were involved in all manner of sin. This is a perfect picture of present day America.

God judged Judah for her sin. Time after time God pleaded with His people to repent but they would not. God is crying out from heaven today for America to repent! God will not allow a nation that murders millions of unborn babies a year to go unjudged. This great nation has turned away from God. Sin abounds on every corner. We have taken the Word of God from the classrooms in our schools. We have turned from God who made-this nation great. One day this nation will stand before God and be judged of her sins. This day may be sooner that we expect, one day soon Jesus Christ is going to return to this world and say "gentlemen it is closing time." The Scripture pleads with us to repent and turn to God while there is still time.

Christians should reread the book of Zephaniah. This is one of the minor Prophetic books of the Old Testament that is seldom read today. Zephaniah's message is full of meaning. It pictures the protecting hand of God. This prophet was the great grandson of King Hezekiah the King who found favor with God. Zephaniah was called to preach during the reign of King Josiah. The nation of Judah was sinking even deeper into sin. The chosen people of God had turned away from the Creator who has so wonderfully blessed them.

When a nation turns from God judgment will surely come. This great prophet prophecies the coming judgment of Judah and the fall of Jerusalem. The theme of this book is the day of the Lord. God was going to judge His people because of their wicked sins. Chapter three of Zephaniah tells of us of the sinful condition of God's people. They are described as filthy, rebellious, and polluted.

They are rebellious because they would not submit to the known will of God. They were polluted because of their continuance of living in sin while professing to be living according to God's Word. Jesus speaks of this sin in the twenty-third chapter of Matthew. Judah was also oppressing because of the way she treated the poor, the orphans, and the widows.

The leaders are described as roaring lions. Their great goal was to oppress the people and fill their pockets with gold. The judges are described as envying wolves. Wolves are vicious animals. These judges had no mercy on the people of God. Not only did the leaders and judges bring the judgment of God but also the prophets and the priests. The prophets were those who brought the message of God to His people. These men had become treacherous. Instead of proclaiming the-Word of-God they had begun to act hypocritically and to pillage the people.

Even the priests had turned away from God. The priests were those who went before God to intercede for the sins of the people. Now they had polluted the sanctuary and done violence to the Law. The word polluted means that they had made common or unclean that which is sacred, holy, or dignified. These men openly rebelled against the teachings of the Word of God.

Reading this Scripture is like reading today's newspaper. This natural man continues in his in. This chapter is an echo from the past sins of America. Greed and sin are widespread in our government today. God will not tolerate the sins of His people. The Prophet writes: Zephaniah 3: 5-7.

> The just Lord is in the midst of her; he will not do iniquity; every morning doth he bring his judgement to light, he faileth not; but the unjust knoweth no shame. I have cut off the nations, their towers are desolate; I made their streets waste, that none passeth by; their cities are destroyed, so that there is no man, that there is no inhabitant.[44]

God brought to light the sins of the nation. We are told in the Word of God that man's sin will find him out. Man cannot hid his sin forever. There comes a day when the darkest sins of man's heart comes to light. God offered His chosen people the forgiveness of sins if they would only repent and turn back to Him. They would not listen to the voice of their God. They felt no shame in their corrupted ways. Because of their sin of unbelief and rebellion God's judgment came upon them.

Our nation today is following the same course of Judah. The message of God is going out today for men to repent, Men blinded by Satan continue to march on in their sin toward a devil's hell. One can only wonder how long will it be before a holy and righteous God brings this nation to its knees because of their sins. The Bible tells us when this judgment will be. Revelation 1:1 introduces us to this book of the Bible.

> The Revelation of Jesus Christ, which gave God unto him, to show unto his servants things which must shortly come to pass; and he sent and signified it by his angel unto his servant, John.[45]

Jesus is the center of the ages. He is the Alpha and Omega, the beginning and the ending. Jesus is the central person of the Bible. The Bible speaks of many men and things. It speaks of angels and devils. It tells of the sinfulness of man. The sins of man and Satan are recorded for all the universe to see. Through all the sin and shame that men have traveled, there comes one glorious person to redeem this fallen creature made in the image of God.

The final book of the Bible speaks of the glorious returning of Jesus Christ to this earth. On that great day He will put an end to the devil. On that day the nations of this world will bow their knees to the Prince of life, Jesus Christ.

As stated above we live in an age where sin is rampant. Drugs and alcohol are everywhere. Families are breaking up at an alarming rate. Murder, rape, and all manner of evil is being done without shame or remorse. Millions of people have become their own gods. They stand in their sin and deny the very existence of Almighty God. We live in perhaps the most ungodly age this world has ever passed through. Millions upon millions of unborn babies have been murdered in their mothers womb, and the government of this great nation nods its head in approval of this mass murder. This echoes the horror of Herod's slaying of the innocent children at the birth of Jesus. Matthew 2: 16-18.

> *Then Herod when he saw that he was mocked of the wise men, was exceedingly angry, and sent forth, and slew all the children that were in Bethlehem, and in all its borders, from two years old and under, according to the time which he had diligently inquired of the wise men. Then was fulfilled that which was spoken by Jeremiah, the prophet saying. In Rama was there a voice heard, lamentation, and weeping, and great mourning, Rachel weeping for her children, and would not be comforted, because they are not.*[46]

Oh how the heart of God must be bleeding with death of these unborn babies. Is it any wonder why when John finished the book of Revelation that he fell on his knees and cried for our Blessed Lord to come. Did not Jesus say that if He did not shortened the days of this world that no flesh would be saved. Mark 13: 20.

> *And except the Lord had shortened those days, no flesh should be saved; but for the elects sake, whom He hath chosen. He hath shortened the days.*[47]

When the time is at hand Jesus Christ the Son of God will return to this earth. On that day it will be closing time for Satan and all whose who not know Jesus Christ as Lord and Savior. There are some who say that they will never bow their knee to Jesus or ever confess Him as Lord. This man is in for a rude awakening. Paul writes in the Book of Philippians 2: 9-11.

> Wherefore, God hath highly exalted him, and given him a name which is above every name. That at the name of Jesus every knee shall bow, of things under the earth, and that every tongue should confess that Jesus Christ is Lord, to the glory of God, the Father.[48]

May that day soon come quickly. When Jesus comes there will be no need for Counselors of any kind. The Counseling profession in that day will become obsolete.

Chapter X

The Hard Side of the Human Experience

Our Lord does not expect His servants to water down the Word of God. We are not to compromise the message of God. Above all the pastor\counselor should never preach a pie in the sky religion. Many of the pie in the sky preachers today are preaching a terrible heresy. They promise that once a person exercises his faith he will automatically find; himself in a bed of roses. The Bible does not teach any of this—nonsense. Once a person becomes a Christian and gives his life to Jesus Christ it does not mean that all suffering ceases. Nor does it mean that the poor of this world will be no more. Jesus tells us that this world will always be filled with the poor. John 12:8.

> For the poor always ye have with you; but me ye have not always.[49]

> I Peter 3: 17

> For it is better, if the will of God be so, that ye suffer for well doing, than evil doing.[50]

This certainly does not sound like the pie in the sky preacher or counselor.

The Old Testament Prophet Habakkuk records one of the greatest confessions of faith ever uttered in the Bible. Habakkuk 3: 17-19.

Although the fig tree shall not blossom, neither shall fruit be in the vines; the labour of the olive shall fail, and the fields shall yield no meat; the flock shall be cut off from the fold, and there be no herd in the stalls; Yet I will rejoice in the Lord, I will joy in the God of my salvation. The Lord God is my strength, and He will make my feet like hinds feet, and He will make me to walk upon mine high places. To the chief singer on my stringed instruments.[51]

This is the Old Testament version of what the Apostle Paul writes in the New Testament. Philippians 4: 11-13.

Not that I speak in respect of want; for I have learned, in whatsoever state I am, therewith to be content. I know both how to be abashed, and I know how to abound; everywhere in all things I am instructed both to be full and to be hungry, both to abound and to suffer need. I can do all. things through Christ which strength me.[52]

Habakkuk was man with a burdened heart. This book should be read and studied by every Christian. The Prophet of God was a troubled man. The people of Israel were living in sin. For their great sins against God judgment came upon them. God used a godless and wicked nation to judge His people.

Habakkuk in his grief cried out, "Although the fig tree shall not blossom, neither shall fruit be in the vines; the labor of the olive shall fail, and the fields yield no food; the flock shall be cut off from the fold, and there shall be no herd in the stalls." This is a picture of a man that is hurting.

This verse of Scripture clearly teaches that the people of God are subject to suffering. This is a picture of a man that is on rock bottom.

The pie in the sky preacher\counselor does not consider Bible passages such as these. He is not concerned with the Word of God. He is not even concerned with the people who come to him for help He is concerned with his own selfish desires.

Anyone who does not preach the truth of the gospel are not serving the Lord Jesus Christ. They are serving their own bodies. Pie in the sky preachers fall into this category. The Apostle Paul writes concerning these: Romans 16: 17-18.

> Now I beseech you, brethren, mark them who cause divisions and offenses contrary to the doctrine which he has learned; and avoid them. For they are such serve not our Lord Jesus Christ but their own body, and by good words and fair speeches deceive the hearts of the innocent.[53]

We are certainly living in a day of pie in the sky religion. We are bombarded everyday with this false teaching. We hear so-called prophets of God cry out their ungodly message everyday. We are told that God desires that all be wealthy and drive big shiny cars. It is not God's will that all people live in million dollars homes. Some even go so far to say that if you do not have prosperity in your life it is because you are not living a life for God.

The Bible does not teach this nonsense. There are many of God's children who has taken for a ride. There people in the world who have real problems. They are hurting deep in their soul. The answer to their is the Lord Jesus Christ. They do not need anything else. Only God can cure the woes of mortal man.

Many of hurting people are like sheep who are being devoured by a raging wolf. We hear certain men say to them a love offering and God will surely bless you. I will be most happy to pray for you. Please send your love offering of faith and receive your blessing from God. In most cases what happens is that the poor suffering soul sends his money and continues in his suffering. While the false prophet smiles all the way to the bank. There are several serious errors in this pie in the sky religion today. First, God does not expect for His servants to have to beg for money. God has promised to meet our every need. Consider the words of our Lord: Matthew 6: 28-34.

> And why are ye anxious for raiment? Consider the lilies of the field, how they grow, they toil not, neither do they spin, and yet I say unto you that even Solomon, in all his glory was not arrayed like one of these. Wherefore, if God so clothe the grass of the field, which today is, and tomorrow is cast

*in the oven, shall he not much more clothe you, O ye of little
faith? Therefore, be not anxious saying. What shall we eat?
What shall we drink? Or with what shall we clothed? For
after all these things do the Gentiles seek. For your heavenly
Father knoweth that ye have need of all these things. But
seek ye first the kingdom of God, and His righteousness, and
all things shall be added to you. Be, therefore, not anxious
about tomorrow; for tomorrow will be anxious for the things
of itself. Sufficient unto the day is its self.*[54]

Matthew chapter twelve records our Lord sending out of the
twelve Apostles. The Lord gave these men a wonderful ministry. They
were given power to heal the sick, cleanse the lepers, raise the dead,
and to cast out demons. The Lord reminded them that the power they
had was freely to them by God. They were to make no charge or ask
for any gifts from the people. In fact the Savior commanded them
not to take their purses. They should not worry about silver or gold
or even the shoes on their feet. Our blessed Savior promised that the
God of glory would provide their every need.

Our Lord also says something concerning those His servants
minister to. The Word of God is precious. Christ told His servants:
Luke 9: 5.

*And whosoever shall not receive you, nor hear your words,
when ye depart out of that house or city, shake off the dust
of your feet for a testimony against them.*[55]

There are two things clear from this passage. God's people are to
faithful in the preaching of the Word. God's people are to faithful in
supporting the ministry of God's servants. Our God does not expect
His servants to water down the Word. We are not to compromise the
message of God. Above all the preacher or Counselor should never
preach a pie in the sky religion.

The Scripture clearly teaches that the pie in the sky preacher\
counselor is not preaching for the glory of God. These people are
noted for their sweet sounding words. It is easy to understand how
they are so successful in deceiving the innocent.

The Apostle Paul offers helpful information concerning these false Teachers. The Holy Spirit moved Paul to say:

> And this I say, lest any man should beguile you with enticing words. For though I be absent in the flesh, yet am I with you in the spirit, joying and beholding your order, and the steadfastness of your faith in Christ. As ye have therefore Christ Jesus the Lord, so walk ye in Him: Rooted and built up in Him, and stablished in the faith, as ye have been taught, abounding therein with thanksgiving. Beware lest any man spoil you through vain philosophy and deceit, after the tradition of men, after the rudiments of the world, and not after Christ.[56]

The word beguile as used here is from the Greek word "paralogizomai" which means to deceive by false reasoning. These false preachers\counselors are deceiving the people of God. The word "enticing" means to lure by bait, persuasive speech. The Bible tells us to be on guard against these false teachings. They are the messengers of Satan. Satan has given them the ability to deceive.

The Scripture clearly teaches that their ministry is one of philosophy and vain deceit, after the tradition of men, after the rudiments of the world, and not after the Lord Jesus Christ.

In the confusion of these days we need to remember the words of Habakkuk 3: 17-19. There will be times in the Christian life when our days will be dark. Satan will attempt to hinder the Christian at every turn. However, dark days should not make us despair. We are to be like the of old who cried out: Habakkuk 3: 18.

> I will joy in the God of my salvation. The Lord God is my strength.[57]

The Bible encourages people to depend upon God. The Lord Jesus Christ invites all to come to Him. He promises to meet our every need. Not only will Christ meet our every need He will give us our hearts desire. He alone can fill a broken heart with the joy of God. Christ Jesus tells us: Matthew 11: 28-30.

Come unto me all that labor and are heavy laden, and I will give you rest. Take my yoke upon you, and learn of me; for I am meek and lowly in heart: and ye shall find rest unto your souls. For my yoke is easy, and my burden is light.[58]

It would be a wonderful thing if we could always remain on the mountain top with Christ Jesus. A mountain in Scripture speaks of a place of special privilege. Luke 9: 27-36 tells of our Lord's transfiguration. It is here that the disciples saw the marvelous glory of the Lord. They would have gladly remained on that mountain with our Savior. It is good to be there with Christ. We need those mountain top experiences with our Lord. It does us good to get away from the cares of this world, and enjoy those sacred moments alone with Christ.

We cannot always remain on the mountain. Verse 37 of Luke chapter nine tells us that the next day Jesus and the disciples came down, and many people were there to meet him. These mountain top experiences with our Lord are to prepare us for what we encounter in the valleys of life below. Sin, sickness, pain and death are around us. Without the presence of Christ we would not be able to cope with this.

In the crowd that met our Savior was a poor troubled father. The man's only son was demon possessed! The man cried out to Jesus for Him to heal his son. We can feel the agony that was in this man's heart. His only son was in bondage to Satan. There are many in this condition today. Many parents today are broken hearted over their children.

This man went to the disciples of Christ and they could not help him. The reason for their failure is found in verse 36 of chapter three of Luke. Instead of feasting on Christ, they were concerned which of them would be the greatest in the kingdom of God. For a moment they took their minds off Christ and became self-centered. When we look to self and not to Christ we are of little value to ourselves an too others.

There is a great lesson in this Scripture. When we face the problems of life we need to go directly to the Lord Jesus Christ. Peter discovered this need. Listen to Peter's words: I Peter 3: 7.

Casting all your cares upon Him; for He careth for you.[59]

Our blessed Savior reaches out and invites all to come unto Him. Again to the words of His great invitation. Matthew 11: 28-30.

> Come unto me, all ye that labor and are heavy laden, and I will give you rest. Take my yoke upon you, and learn of me; for I am meek and lowly in heart, and ye shall rest unto your souls. For my yoke is easy, and my burden is light.[60]

Many people have the mistaken idea that when one becomes a Christian that immediately his life becomes a bed of roses. The Bible does teach this. In fact the Word of God teaches that the children of God will be hated by the world. The world hated our Savior when He walked among men on the earth (John 15: 18). Christ also says that we expect the same. The Apostle John says: I John 3: 13.

> Marvel not my brethren, if the world hate you.[61]

The Bible also teaches that Christians suffer for righteousness sake. Peter writes: I Peter 3: 14-17.

> But and ye suffer for righteousness sake, happy are ye; and be not afraid of their terror, neither be troubled. But sanctify the Lord in your hearts, and be ready always to give an answer to every man that asketh you a reason of the hope that is in you, with meekness and fear, having a good conscience, that, whereas they speak evil of you, as of evildoers, they may be ashamed that falsely accuse your good manner of life in Christ. For it is better, if the will of God be so, that ye suffer for well doing than for evil doing.[62]

We know through the Word that troubles and persecution may come our way. When it comes we are to stand fast in our Lord. He has promised to keep us. Our faith is to remain strong in God. The Bible says that without faith it is impossible to please God (Hebrews 11:6). However, men do not always stand fast in their faith. The Bible is filled with the names of men who in time of trouble their faith waivered. We read of Peter who walked on the water, however, when he took his eyes off Jesus he began to sink. Peter was so like many today. We look at Christ Jesus and then we go our own way. When Peter began to sink he cried out to our Lord. Jesus reached out His blessed hand and brought Peter up. The hand of Christ is still outstretched for sinners to come unto Him.

The great prophet John the Baptist was another who fell into despair. John was put in prison for his preaching (Luke 7: 19-34). John was the forerunner of Christ. He had boldly preached the coming of the Messiah. Now he was in jail and Satan began to create doubts in his in his mind. John sent two of his disciples to Jesus, saying, "art thou he that should come? Or look we for another?"

Our Lord did not answer John in words. He answered in deeds. Luke 7: 21-23.

> And *it that same hour he cured many of their infirmities and agues, and of evil spirits; and that were blind he gave sight. Then Jesus answering, said unto them. Go your way, and tell John what things ye have seen and heard, how the blind see, the lame walk, the lepers are cleansed, the deaf hear, the dead are raised, to the poor the gospel is preached, and blessed is he, whosoever shall not be offended in me.*[63]

Yes troubles will come. There may be many dark days. But Jesus Christ is still on the Throne. May we all put our faith and trust in Him.

Chapter XI

Faith Appears to Fail

In helping counselees overcome their problems the Christian Counselor must depend upon the Holy Spirit of God. Before attempting to counsel lost people the Counselor must present them with the Gospel of Jesus Christ. Lost people can never have true peace and joy without faith in Jesus Christ.

Some will ask why do Christians have problems? Christians are not immune from the pains and heartaches of life. People who know Jesus Christ as Savior are a special target of Satan. In order to overcome the testings of Satan the believer must be armed with the armor of God.

The battle of life must first begin with faith. The Bible teaches that there are two types of faith. There is saving faith and living faith. Saving faith is a gift from God. Paul writes:

> For by grace are ye saved through faith; and that not of yourselves, it is a gift of God, not of works, lest any man should boast.[64]

The very faith that we have to believe in Jesus Christ as Lord and Savior comes from God Himself. All believers have this saving faith.

Now we come to the discussion of living faith. All believers do not have the same measure of living faith. Our Lord speaks of this living faith in the Gospels.

> *If then, God so cloth the grass, which is today in the field, and tomorrow is cast into the oven, how much more will he cloth, O ye of little faith? And seek not what ye shall eat or drink, neither be ye of doubtful mind.[65]*

Some believers are able to face the greatest of trials while others stumble at the first test. This living faith must be exercised by the life of the believer, In order to cope with the problems of this world we need that great living faith.

Many of the Bible's greatest men have failed in time of crisis. Abraham the great man of God failed soon after his call. His life and struggles are given as an example for believers today. We are introduced to the Old Testament saint in the twelfth chapter of Genesis. Though Abraham was a great man of faith that loved he was not immune from sin. None of us! The Christian Counselor must keep this truth before his mind. Genesis 12: 1-3 records the call of Abraham. These verses indicate that Abraham was in Haran. Verse one lets us know that the call had already been while he was in the land of Ur. The call was here reiterated.

In verses 2-3 gives great and wonderful promises to Abraham. Moses the writer of Genesis writes: Genesis 12: 1-3.

> *Now the Lord had said unto Abram, Get thee out of the country, and from thy kindred, and from thy father's house, unto a land that I will show thee; and I will make of thee a great nation, and I will bless thee, and make thy name great; and thou shalt be a blessing. And I will bless them that bless thee, and curse him that curseth thee; and in thee shall of families of the earth be blessed.[66]*

When God made these promises, Abraham had no son. But he did have great faith! His seed would be a great nation. Not only would his seed become a great nation, but it would be a blessing to all people. There is also a warning found in these verses. Those who curse his seed would be cursed of God. The scene has repeated itself through the centuries. Every nation that has persecuted the people of Israel have been judged by God.

In verse four we are told that Abram departs from Haran and journeys to the promised land. The Holy Spirit emphasizes the fact that Abram was 75 years old. By the standards of this world these promises would be almost impossible. However, this was God's doing and he wanted Abram and all who would read this to know it. God had blessed Abram with much wealth and many servants. Abram journeyed to Shechem, a land occupied by the Canaanites. When Abram arrived there he built an altar and worshipped God.

Now this great man's faith begins to waiver. Verses 9-20 record the sad failure of this man of God. Abram did not lose his salvation. However, his living faith begins to crumble. Instead of walking by faith he began to walk by sight. It is easy for people today to fall into this same situation. We begin by noticing verse nine. Abram was in Bethel and in fellowship with God. This verse states that Abram journeyed going on still southward. South here refers to the Negev. Archaeological evidence suggests that there were prosperous settlements in this area at that time. It is important to remember that Egypt lay just southwest of the Negev. The Bible has much to say about Egypt and none of it is good. God wanted Abram in Bethel, however, Abram saw the wealth of the south, and chose it. This was the first mistake of Abram. When man stops walking with God the troubles of this world will drag him down. Now Abram would face many new trials for not walking with God. His faith would now be sorely tested.

We read in the Scriptures that Abram faced many trials in his life. Genesis 12: 10-20 records such a time. God has called Abram to be the father of the Jewish nation. Abram was directed to Bethel where he built an altar and worshipped God. Verse 10 of chapter 12 tells us that there was a great famine in the land. It is said that famines was not uncommon in Palestine. But can you imagine famine in the land of promise! God was testing the faith of Abram. What good is faith if it cannot be tested, and be found standing fast. The Apostle Peter writes: I Peter Is 7.

> That the trial of your faith, being much more precious than of gold that perisheth, though it be tried with fire, might be found unto praise and honor and glory at the appearing of Jesus Christ.[67]

When the famine was grievous, Abram went down to Egypt. This was his first failure. While Abram was in Egypt his testimony was not what it should have been. After walking across the desert sands to the Promised Land, risking his life and substance on the Word of God; Abram now became a man of fear (verse 12). He was afraid he would be killed. He also became selfish. He was concerned with himself than for his wife. Listen to the words of this man of God. Genesis 12:12.

> Therefore, it shall come to pass, when the Egyptians shall see thee, that they shall say, this is his wife: and they will kill me, but they will save thee alive.[68]

When a man's heart is not on God it is on himself. The example of Abram clearly proves this.

Genesis 12: 13 tells us that Abram did not tell the whole truth. He urged Sarah to say that she was his sister. This was partly true for she was indeed his half sister. Genesis 20:12.

> And yet indeed she is my sister, she is the daughter of my father, but not the daughter of my mother; and she became my wife.[69]

However, a half truth equals a whole lie. Abram certainly meant to deceive. We read: Genesis 26:7.

> And the men of the place asked him of his wife; and he said, she is my sister; for he feared to say, she is my wife; lest, said he, the men of the place should kill me for Rebekah; because she was fair to look upon.[70]

The Bible tells us more about lying than any other sin. How can some say then that Abram was not out of the will of God. Abram's folly led to trouble on others. We read that the Lord plagued Pharaoh and his house with great plagues because of Sarah, Abram's wife (verse 17). This verse has a twofold meaning.

1. The judgment of God will fall on many because His servants are not where they should be.

2. No matter where, are in what spiritual condition, God's people still belongs to Him.

The prodigal son of Luke 15 was never out of the father. We are never out of the heart of God! Genesis 12: 18-19 is a sad commentary of Abram. He was rebuked by a heathen king.

> And Pharaoh called Abram, and said, what is this that thou hast done unto me? Why didst thou not tell us she was thy wife? Why saidest thou, she is my sister? So that i might have taken her to be as my wife: now therefore behold thy wife, take her, and go thy way.[71]

It is sad when the lost of this world can tell us that we do not practice what we preach. We need to be imitators of the Lord, not of the world. Our life is to shine and be a good influence on the lost. Genesis 12:21 tells us that Pharaoh sent Abram and his wife away. Abram lost a golden opportunity to tell people about God. Christians should be like Peter in the New Testament when he said. Acts 3:6.

> Silver and gold have I none but what I have I give it unto you.[72]

Abram had a lot to give. Christians today have a lot to give! Believers should always be found in telling the good news of the Gospel of the Lord Jesus Christ.

Chapter XII

Man Crying Out from Within

Since the first man Adam, rebelled against God this world has been filled with sin. Throughout the ages there has been wars and conflicts around the globe. Our Lord Jesus tells us in the book of Matthew 24: 6-7.

> And ye shall hear of wars and rumors of wars; see that ye be not troubled; for all these things must come to pass, but the end is not yet. For nation shall rise against nation, and kingdom against kingdom; and there shall be famines, and-pestilences, and earthquakes, in various places.[73]

No one can deny that we are not in those days now. Trouble is breaking out everywhere.

These are not only the only wars that are raging today. There are wars being fought in the hearts of men. Paul describes part of this great war in the book of Ephesians 6: 12-17.

> For we wrestle not against flesh and blood, but against principalities, against powers, against the rulers of the darkness of this world, against spiritual wickedness in high places. Wherefore, take unto you the whole armor of God, that ye may be able to withstand in the evil day, and having done all, do stand. Stand therefore, having your loins girded about with truth, having on the breastplate of righteousness.

And your feet shod with the preparation of the gospel of peace. Above all, taking the shield of faith, with which ye shall be able to quench the fiery darts of the wicked. And take the helmet of salvation, and the sword of the Spirit, which is the Word of God.[74]

Yes, this battle isn't against men, but against Satan and his demons. Not only is Satan at battle with the lost, but also with the people of God. In fact Satan seems to delight in attacking those who has been washed in the blood of Jesus Christ.

This battle is not ours alone to fight. For God is the captain of our salvation. We read in the book of Hebrews:

For it became Him, for whom are all things, and by whom are all things, in bringing many sons unto glory, to make the captain of their salvation perfect through suffering.[75]

The word "captain" means author or originator. Christ Jesus is the author of our faith. The Lord always leads His people. When the people of God goes into battle, God is there as our leader. Moses the great leader of Israel wrote long ago that : Exodus 14:14.

The Lord shall fight for you, and ye shall hold your peace.[76]

When we face the powers of darkness we indeed stand in the power and might of God. God through the Holy Spirit moved Paul to record those comforting words in Ephesians 6:12. We are indeed to put on the whole armor of God. This will enable us to stand against the wiles (lies) of Satan. The only way man can stand against Satan is through the power of Jesus Christ.

Paul tells us in Ephesians chapter two verses one and two that the unsaved are spiritually dead. They walk according to the wishes of Satan. The sad part is that lost people are not aware of their bondage to Satan. These poor souls are so blinded by the devil that they can't discern spiritual truth. For example drugs and alcohol destroy the body. Thousands die each year from drug overdose, many are children; yet the use of drugs continue. Then there are those who sell drugs and alcohol. They will often say, "Have a drink or snort, it will make the blues go away." This drink or snort will only cause more misery. Those folks who sell this do not care about the user. They could care less if he lived or died. Their only care is the money they make. This is ever the purpose of Satan.

People can set free from this bondage. The way of escape is through the Lord Jesus Christ. The greatest thrill a person will ever have is knowing that he has the peace of God in his life. People are struggling with inner turmoil need to ask Christ to come into their heart and set them free. People need to be honest with themselves and God.

The believer is not immune from the struggles of life. The seventh chapter of Romans records the strife of the two natures of man. This has been called the most terrible tragedy in all literature. Set aside the seventh chapter of Romans most of man's problems seem next to nothing. It has been said that this chapter should always be printed in letters of blood. Here Paul reveals the passions, fear, terror, and pity of his inner soul. Here heaven and hell meet in eternal conflict. This great man of God wrestles with his old sin nature. Listen to the cries of this man's heart as he calls out to God. Romans 7: 15-25. (TLB)

> *I don't understand myself at all, for I really want to do what is right, bat I can't. I do what I don't want to do what I hate. I know perfectly well that what I am doing is wrong, and my bad conscience proves that I agree with these laws I am breaking. But I can't help myself, because I am no longer doing it. It is sin inside me that is stronger than I am that makes me do these things. I know I am rotten through and through so far as my old sin nature is concerned. So matter which way I turn I can't make myself do right. I want to but I can't. When I want to do good, I don't; and when I try not to do wrong. I do it anyway. Now if I am doing what I don't want to, it is plain where the trouble is; sin still has me in its evil grasp. It seems to be a fact of life that when I want to do what is right, I inevitably do what is wrong. I love to do God's will so far as my new nature is concerned, but it is something else deep within me, in my lower nature, that is at war with my mind and wins the fight and makes me a slave to the sin that is still within me. In my mind I want to God's*

willing servant but instead I find myself still enslaved to sin.
So you see how it is; my new life tells me to do right, but
the old nature that is still inside me loves to sin. Oh, what
a terrible predicament I'm in! Who will free me from my
slavery to this deadly lower nature? Thank God! It has been
done by Jesus Christ our Lord. He has set me free.[77]

The seventh chapter of Romans is not about the struggles of the lost. This struggle concerns the deliverance of the believer. This chapter is not about pardon. The saved are pardoned at the moment of conversion. This chapter centers on the saved man who is struggling with the old sin nature.

When the sinner is saved a great transformation takes place in his life. Ephesians 2:1 tells us that lost people are spiritually dead. There is absolutely no life within them. They are walking in darkness under the bondage of Satan.

It is God who gives life to the lost of this world. Ephesians 2:8 tells us that we are saved by the grace of God through faith. Man can't save himself. He will never be able to do enough good works to merit God's favor. Only by the grace of God through the blood of Jesus Christ can be saved.

Jesus calls our conversion experience the new birth in John 3:3.

Jesus answered, and said unto him, verily, verily, I say unto
thee, except a man be born again, he cannot see the kingdom
of God.[78]

This is our spiritual birth that comes from God. Unless a man receives this spiritual birth he can never have peace with God.

The new birth is the most joyful experience a man will ever have. Not only does God save. He comes to indwell the body of the believer. Each believer has the Holy Spirit of God within him. Note the words of Paul. Romans 8:9.

But ye are not flesh but in the Spirit, if so be that the Spirit
of God dwell in you. Now if any man have not the Spirit of
Christ, he is none of His.[79]

There are some who teach that people can be saved and not have the Holy Spirit in them. This is a false teaching that is not found in the Word of God. Romans 8:9 along with John 14:23 clearly states that if God's Spirit is not in man, he is not saved.

John 14:23 reveals more precious truth.

> Jesus answered, and said unto him, if a man love me, he will keep my words; and my Father will love him, and we will come unto him, and make our abode with Him.[80]

Christ Jesus says that not only will the Spirit abide in the believer but also the Father and the Son. Note the word "we" of this verse. It speaks of the Trinity of God (Father, Son, and Holy Spirit).

Now we come to the seventh chapter of Romans again and ask, how can it be? What causes this great struggle in the believer? The struggle comes because of the two natures. When we are saved God imparts to us the new nature, His nature. The old nature is not taken away, it remains with us. It will be with us as long as we remain in this earthly body of clay. Throughout life the believer will have control the old sin nature that beats in his chest. This battle was so strong in Paul's life that he cried out, "Oh wretched man that I am." "Who shall deliver me from this body of death." The only one who is able to deliver is God (Romans 7:25).

This does not mean that believers have the privilege to continue to practice sin! God calls His people to holy living. It is true that we will have struggles and trials. Galatians 5:17 tells us of the struggle the Spirit will have with our fleshly nature. We can overcome the flesh, the sin nature, through the power of God. We can have sweet victory in our lives if we follow the commandment of God given in Galatians 5:16.

> This I say then, walk in the Spirit, and ye shall not fulfill the lusts of the flesh.[81]

Yes, we are indeed in a great war. On one side we have the devil and his demons to deal with. On the other side we have the old sin nature. This fleshly nature of our heart is fertile ground for Satan the devil. In order to overcome him we must walk in the Spirit. Though our battle is great we must not despair. The Captain of our salvation, The Lord Jesus Christ, has crushed the power of Satan. Satan is no longer an invincible foe.

Genesis 3:15 records the first prophecy of Satan's defeat. We are told that Satan would bruise the heel of Jesus. When Jesus was on the cross for our sins Satan reached out with all his power. He summoned all the powers of hell and sank his fangs deep in the heel of our blessed Savior. He was greatly mistaken! While Satan's fangs was in the heel of Jesus, our Lord crushed the old serpent's head! Jesus pushed all His weight down upon the devil's head and now is defeated. He has no power over God or His people.

The victory of the Lord Jesus was complete. The devil has been bound by the blood of Jesus Christ. Consider those precious words of Christ. Mark 3: 22-29.

> And He called unto him, and said unto them in parables. How can Satan cast out Satan. And if a kingdom be divided against itself, that kingdom cannot stand. And if a house be divided against itself, that house cannot stand. And if Satan rise up against himself, and be divided he cannot stand, but hath an end. No man can enter into a strong's man house, and spoil his goods, except he will first bind the strong man; and then he will spoil his house. Verily I say unto you, all sins shall be forgiven unto the sons of men, and blasphemies with which they shall blaspheme; but he that shall blaspheme against the Holy Ghost hath never forgiveness but is in danger of eternal damnation.[82]

Christ Jesus is the strong man that has bound the power of Satan. Jesus Christ is now setting men free by the thousands.

Not only has the power of the devil been bound, it has also been restricted and restrained. Paul tells us in II Thessalonians 2:6 that the work of Satan is now being hindered by the Holy Spirit of God. The Scripture also teaches that Satan has also been rendered powerless over believers. The writer of Hebrews records: Hebrews 2:14.

Fore as much, then as the children are partakers of flesh and blood, he also himself likewise took part of the same that through death he might destroy him that-had the power of death, that is death.[83]

The Scripture also teaches that the devil has already been judged by God. Satan's eternal home is the Lake of Fire. He is a loser. There is no hope for him. People who follow Satan need to realize his destiny and turn from their sins and seek the forgiveness of Almighty God.

Even the works of Satan have been destroyed. The victory of Jesus Christ on the cross was complete in every way. The Apostle John writes: I John 3:8.

For this purpose the Son of God was manifested, that He might destroy the works of the devil.[84]

Yes, Satan is a defeated foe. People can be set free from his grip. God in His wonderful grace is redeeming men to Himself. The grace of God is beyond our human imagination. There is so much of God that we can't understand or comprehend. However, there is much that is as clear as crystal. One such truth is that Satan can't touch the child of God. John makes this truth very clear. I John 5:18.

We know that whosoever is born of God sinneth not, but he that is begotten of God keepeth himself, and that wicked one touched him not.[85]

Satan may throw fiery darts but he can' put his dirty hands upon God's children. The believer should never be afraid of Satan. The saved are the blood of Jesus. We are in the hands of God and Satan can't touch us! So many declare that Satan is on our back. They say they can't shake Satan's grip. This is not what the Word of God says. The Bible says resist the devil, and he will flee from you. (James 4:7). If you want the devil to be gone, resist him, rebuke him in the name of the Lord. He is a coward and will flee from you. Those who say Satan will not leave them alone are not doing what God tells us to do. Satan's power has been broken by the blood of Jesus.

Chapter XIII

Isolation

We live in a fast and changing world that has caused many problems. Loneliness, a common problem has been described by many as one of the most universal sources of human suffering. Everyday we meet people who feel alone in this cold world. There are millions living out the old Hank Williams song, "I'm so lonesome I could cry." Gary Collins describes loneliness as:

> The painful awareness that we lack meaningful contact with others. It involves a feeling of inner emptiness which can be accompanied by sadness, discouragement, a sense of isolation, restlessness, anxiety and intense desire to be wanted and needed by someone.[86]

God did not intend for man to be alone and lonely. We read in the book of Genesis 2:18.

> And the Lord said, it is not good that the man should be alone; I will make an help meet for him.[87]

God in His wisdom knew that man could not cope with being alone. God created a woman from the rib of Adam and brought her unto him. They were to be fruitful and multiply and fill the earth. Throughout the Bible we read of the need for man to commune with God and other people.

The Bible is filled with the names of men who have felt alone and deserted. On the way back to Bethel, Jacob was left alone (Genesis 32:24). He was lonely and afraid because of the fear of man. Moses the chosen man of God to lead His people from bondage also had moments of loneliness. He gave his entire life to the service of God and to his people only to have his own flesh and blood complain of his leadership. Elijah became afraid of a heathen Queen and fled for his life. At Mt. Horeb he cried out to God that he was the only prophet left and that he was afraid for his life (I Kings 19:14).

We read of our blessed Savior in the Garden of Gethsemane being alone. While his holy soul was in agony praying to' the Father His three closest friends were asleep a few yards away. The next day He was nailed to a Roman cross for the sins of the world. Matthew records that awesome day in such detail. He states that Jesus cried out: Matthew 27:46.

My God, my God, why has thou forsaken me.[88]

Yes, Jesus Christ suffered alone on that cross. Even God the Father turned His head away. The reason was for our sins.

There are multitudes of people today suffering from loneliness. There are many reasons why people are lonely. People are lonely as the result of the death of a loved one. Very few in life want to face the future without their lifelong partner. There have been stories told of how a spouse would grieve themself to death after the loss of a loved one.

Children often feel alone because of a poor relationship with their parents. Children need to be told they are loved. When they are not you will usually have a lonely child. We could go on with the causes of loneliness. The world is filled with lonely people seeking to find help for their troubled souls.

Loneliness like sin always produces bad side effects. People who are lonely will often isolates themselves like Elijah did when he fled from Jezebel (I Kings 19). Or perhaps people will respond in the way of David or Job. These two great men referred themselves as worms Job cries out: Job 25:6.

How much less man, who is a worm, and the son of man, who is a worm?[89]

David utters almost the same cry: Psalm 22:6.

But I am a worm, and no man; a reproach of men, and despised by the people.[90]

Most all Bible scholars including myself consider the word of David to be Messianic prophecy. The wonderful twenty-second Psalm of Old Testament Prophecy of the suffering of our Savior on Calvary's cross. This indeed proves that our Lord and Savior suffered from loneliness. He was indeed touched with the same testing as we were. The writer of Hebrews sums it up best when he wrote: Hebrews 4: 15.

For we have not an high priest who cannot be touched with the feelings of our infirmities, but was in all points tempted like as we are, yet without sin.[91]

There are times when most all people feel like failures. I think there were times when Moses felt like a failure. The Prophet Jeremiah's loneliness was vent out in mourning. When we read the book of Lamentations we discover that was deep in the heart of this man of God.

Praise the name of God there is a way to prevent and cure loneliness. People should not spend all their time brooding over their problems. If one is lonely he needs to confess it to God as David did. King David cried out: Psalm 25:16.

Turn unto me, and have mercy upon me, for I am desolate and afflicted.[92]

God is concerned with our well being. People should also remember that there are simply some things that cannot be changed. Solomon wrote long ago: Ecclesiastes 8:6.

Because to every purpose there time and judgment, therefore the misery of man is great upon him.[93]

Man cannot bring someone back from the dead. Therefore, death must be accepted. Most important of all man needs to claim the promises of God. We are told in Hebrews 13:5 that God will never leave us or forsake us. When God is with you there is no reason to be lonely. If we are to overcome these emotions and feelings of loneliness, we must put our faith and trust in Him and claim the victory that He has given each of us.

I am neither pro nor anti medicine, but I am for whatever works. Obviously, a person is better off if they can get along without medication. However, there are illnesses/conditions which necessitate medication. In the Book of Jeremiah, God says, "is there no balm in Gilead then why are not my people healed?" God is our medicine and under the right conditions, He can heal better than any medication. This does not imply that this writer does not believe that a person should not take prescribed medications, if a medical doctor has determined that this is necessary, then by all means, a person should follow their doctor's advice.

Chapter XIV

Experiencing Spiritual Nutrition in Christ

The world is filled with millions of people who have been touched by the hand of Jesus Christ. When God saves a sinner a great transformation takes place in the life and the heart of the individual. Jesus speaks of this experience as the new birth in the third chapter of the Gospel of John. When the person is saved he begins to grow in Christ. Paul sums it best in the book of Romans 12:1,2.

> J beseech you therefore, brethren, by the mercies of God, that ye present your bodies a living sacrifice, holy, acceptable unto God, which is your reasonable service. And be not conformed to this world, but be ye transformed by the renewing of your mind, that ye may prove what is that good, and acceptable, and perfect, will of God.[94]

Not everyone who hears the Gospel of Christ responds in the same manner. There are those who hear the Word of God and are saved. Their life becomes one of close fellowship with God. There are others who hear the Gospel of Christ and rejects His offer of eternal life and peace with Him. In order to better understand the effects of the Gospel on different people our Lord gave us the parable of the seed and the sower. This parable is recorded in the first three Gospels. However, Matthew offers more detail. The parable of the seed and sower will be our basic study for this chapter. God has a message for men today that is found in this parable. The Apostle Matthew writes: Matthew 13: 1-23.

The same day went Jesus out of the house, and sat by the seaside. And great multitudes were gathered together unto Him, so that He went into a ship, and sat; and the whole multitude stood on the shore. And He spoke many things unto them in parables, saying. Behold a sower went forth to sow; and when he sowed, some of the seeds fell by the wayside, and the fowls came and devoured them. Some fell upon stony places, where they had not earth; and forth with they sprung up, because they had no deepness of earth. And when the sun was up, they were scorched; and because they had no root, they withered away. And some fell among thorns; and the thorns sprang up, and choked them. But other seeds fell into good ground, and brought forth fruit, some an hundredfold, some sixty-fold, some thirtyfold. Who hath ears to hear, let him hear. And the disciples came, and said unto him. Why speakest thou unto them in parables? He answered and said unto them. Because it is given unto you to know the mysteries of the kingdom of heaven, but unto them is not given. For whosoever hath, to him shall be given, and he shall have more abundance; but whosoever hath not, from him shall be taken away even what he hath. Therefore speak I to them in parables, because they seeing, see not; and hearing, they hear not, neither do they understand. And in them is fulfilled the prophecy of Isaiah, which saith, By hearing, ye shall hear and shall not understand; and seeing, ye shall see and shall not perceive; For this people's heart is become gross, and their ears are dull of hearing, and their eyes they have closed, lest at any time they should see with their eyes, and hear with their ears, and should understand with their heart, and should be converted, and I should heal them. But blessed are your eyes, for they see; and your ears, for they hear. For verily I say unto you that many prophets and righteous men have desired to see those things which ye see, and have not seen them; and to hear those things which ye hear, and have not heard them. Bear, therefore, the parable of the sower. When

> anyone hearth the word of the kingdom, and understandeth
> it no, then cometh the wicked one, and catcheth away that
> which was sown in his heart. This is he that the heareth the
> Word and immediately with joy receiveth it; Yet hath he not
> root in himself, but endureth for a while; for when tribulation
> or persecution ariseth because of the Word, immediately he
> is offended. Be also that received seed among the thorns is
> he that heareth the Word; and the care of this age, and the
> deceitfulness of riches, choke the Word, and he becometh
> unfruitful. But he that received seed in the good ground is
> he that heareth the Word, and understandeth it, who also
> beareth fruit, and bringeth forth, some an hundred fold,
> some sixty, some thirty.[95]

The parable of the seed and the sower should be a warning of an encouragement to all who labor in the Gospel. Not all who hear the Gospel will be saved. Some will hear the Word and ponder it in their hearts and minds. But the Word will take no root and they shall go their own way. Some will openly reject the claims of Christ. Many people will walk the Church aisles and profess faith in Christ, but they never receive Christ Jesus into their heart. They merely professed Christ with their mouth but did not believe in their heart unto salvation.

It is the believer's place to sow the Word of God. Solomon writes in Ecclesiastes 11:6.

> In the morning sow thy seed, and in the evening withhold not
> thine hand; for thou knowest not which shall prosper, either
> this or that, or whether they both shall be alike good.[96]

We have no way of knowing who will receive the Word into their hearts and be saved. We know that the Word of God is incorruptible and abides forever. The Apostle Peter writes: I Peter 1:23.

> Being born, not of corruptible seed, but of incorruptible, by
> the Word of God, which liveth and abideth forever.[97]

Though many reject the Word of God it will accomplish the purpose of God. Isaiah the prophet writes: Isaiah 55:11.

So shall my Word be that goeth forth out of my mouth; it shall not return unto me void, but it shall accomplish that which I please, and it shall prosper in the thing whereto I sent it.[98]

God also promises that those who hear the Word in faith will be saved. Christ Jesus says: 5:24.

Verily, verily, I say unto you. Be that heareth my Word, and believeth on him that sent ne, hath everlasting life, and shall not come into condemnation, but is passed from death unto life.[99]

The Word of God tests as well as saves. All men should examine themselves to see if they are in the faith. We are to prove or test ourselves. We are to simply take an honest look into our heart and life. The individual needs to make sure that Jesus Christ is in his heart and that they are making a false profession.

Where possible the believer is to break up fallow ground and not sow among the thorns. The prophet Jeremiah writes: Jeremiah 4:3.

For thus saith the Lord to the men of Judah and Jerusalem, break up your fallow ground, and not sow among thorns.[100]

On the other hand he is to be instant in season and out of season. The Apostle Paul wrote to the young Timothy stating: II Timothy 4:1,2.

I charge thee, therefore, before God, and the Lord Jesus Christ, who shall judge the living and the dead at his appearing and his kingdom: Preach the Word; be diligent in season, out of season; reprove, rebuke, exhort with all long suffering and doctrine.[101]

The believer who sows the Word will often find some of the seed falling on cold unprepared hearts, only to be devoured by Satan and his demons.

The first three verses of Luke chapter eight serve as an introduction to the parable of the sower. Our Lord had just left the home of Simon the Pharisee. Simon was a cold hearted, self righteous man. He was a religious man but was far from the kingdom of God.

While in the home of Simon a woman who was a great sinner fell at the feet of Jesus. She began to wash His feet with her tears. She dried them with the hair of her head. She was a woman who came to Jesus and found salvation for her troubled soul.

Our Lord leaves the home of Simon and goes throughout every city and village preaching and teaching the Word of God. What a wonderful testimony we have in verse two. When we receive the Word of God and are saved we should show the power of our redeemed lives. Jesus was preaching the Gospel. Before He began His ministry He worked in the carpenter's shop to support Himself. Now He depends on the gifts of believers to support His great work. What a joy and blessing to give to the work of our Lord.

When it was time to pay taxes our Savior had no money. He sent Peter to catch fish. When Peter brought the fish up out of the water the tax money was in its mouth. One day the Pharisees asked, "Is it lawful to give tribute to Caesar?" Instead of taking a coin out of his pocket, He asked for someone to show him a penny. Yes, Jesus entered into our world of poverty to feel our pain and sorrow. Where did the money come from to support our Lord? It came from these devoted women who ministered to Him."

There are many women who ministered to the needs of Christ Jesus. Three are mentioned by name, Mary Magdalene, Joanna, the wife of Chuza, Herod's steward; and Susanna. Mary had been under the terrible bondage of Satan. Our Lord had cast seven demons out of her. Now she is set free from Satan and sin and is found ministering to Our blessed Savior. Then we read of Joanna, the wife of Chuza, Herod's steward. She gladly turned her back on the riches of this world to follow Christ. Susanna and many others turned from the cares of this world to follow Christ.

As Jesus stood preaching many people gathered together and come to Him out of every city as He spoke to them in parables. There is a Divine drawing power that comes from Christ. It is true that the Priests, Pharisees and Scribes would not believe on Him. They did not like His message or His claims. But they could not resist being drawn into His presence. They came and heard and went away into their own lustful desires. So it is with many people today. How unlike those faithful women of verse two who came to minister unto Jesus.

As our Lord spoke this parable He was at the seaside. Perhaps He looked up and saw a sower sowing his seed on the hillside. Our Lord drew His parables from everyday life. This is what makes them so fresh and appealing to human hearts today.

As the sower went forth to sow his seed some fell by the wayside; and it was trodden down. The birds of the air came and devoured it. The sower spreads his precious seed as he walks up and down his field. So much of the seed is lost. Some of the seed fell among thorns; and the thorns sprang up with it, and choked it. Some seed fell on good ground and sprang up, and bore fruit and hundredfold. And when Jesus has said these things, He cried, "He that hath ears to hear, let him hear." It is impossible to hear with the ear but never let the Word of God get into the heart.

They hear with their ear but the Word of God does not dwell in their hearts.

When they were alone the disciples asked Christ what the parable meant. Even the twelve were slow to understand. Jesus said unto them: Luke 8:10.

> Onto you it is given to know the mysteries of the kingdom
> of God; but to others in parables, that seeing they might not
> see, and hearing they might not understand.[102]

Some people find this a very hard saying. Some even find fault with our Lord. God forbid! Jesus is saying, if you want to know him you will. If one comes to Christ in faith He will give you understanding. Our Lord will reveal precious secrets to those who come to Him with and honest heart before Him. When people give their lives to Jesus Christ they begin to feast at His table which is always filled.

As we study the parable of the seed and the sower we do not need to depend on our own understanding. Our Lord explains this parable to us. The seed is the Word of God. The sower is the Son of God. The soil is the human heart. The seed is the Word of God. When we preach, teach, or witness we are to sow the Word of God. We are not to give our thoughts or ideas. Sermons today are just that. There are very few preachers today who are sowing the Word of God. The Christian world man not want to hear this but it is true. So many today talk about everything under the sun except the Word of God. Many Christian Counselors attempt to counsel hurting people with human philosophy. They discount the Holy Scripture all together. To many so-called Christian Counselors the Bible has become old fashioned and out of date while their counselees starve for the Word of God.

First, we have the seed that fell by the wayside. These are those who hear the Word of God, then comes the devil and takes the Word from their hearts lest they should believe and be saved. What a sad picture. These people come to Church. They listen casually to the Word. They may even pay close attention for a little while. Soon they become interested in the things of the world. These people have been called the wayside hearers. They hear the Word of God but receive no life. The people have cold hearts. In fact their hearts are hard as the highway. The seed cannot penetrate and germinate. There are so many in the Churches today. People will ask, why is the Church having so many problems today? The reason is that some of the members are only wayside hearers. Satan takes the Word of God from them.

Then we have the stony ground hearer. These when they hear, receive the Word with joy; and believe, and these have no root, who for a while believe, and in time of testing fall away. Did you hear what the Savior said? When they heard they received the Word with joy but they have no root and when trouble comes they fall away. Note the word "joy." Can it be that when people receive the Word with joy at first that it is not a good sign. To be truly saved one must repent of sin and confess faith in Christ Jesus. The sinner must confess his sins or he will not be saved. When one first realizes that he is a sinner this does not bring joy. When a person realizes that he is lost and going to hell there is no joy in his heart. This person feels miserable! When people see their deep need for Christ it is when they have a broken heart. God's way is to wound that He may heal.

Listen to the words of God recorded in the Book of Deuteronomy 32:39.

See now that I, even I, am he, and there is no god with me:
I kill, and I make alive; I wound, and I heal; neither is there
any that can deliver out of my hand.[103]

Next we have the seed that fell among the thorns. When they have heard, go forth, and are choked with cares and riches, and the pleasures of this life. These people bring no fruit to perfection. What a sad picture! These people are interested in the Gospel only to a small extent. However, they are far more interested in the things of this life such as pleasure seeking, money making, and many other worldly cares. The seed is in, on, and down but it does not come up. There is absolutely no fruit. There are three things in this verse that we need to note. They are, "worldly cares," "riches," and "pleasures of life." This reminds us of the rich young ruler who came to Jesus in search of eternal life. This young rich man was not willing to give up the pleasures of this world for life eternal. Each individual person must make a decision. They can have life with Christ or the temporary pleasures of this world, heaven or hell. There is no middle ground. We cannot serve two masters.

Now we come to the good ground hearer. What a blessing he is! Listen again to the words of Jesus concerning these people. St. Luke 8:15.

But that on the good ground are they who, in an honest and
good heart, having heard the word keep it, and bring forth
fruit with patience.[104]

The Bible also tells us that the human heart is wicked. Jeremiah the prophet wrote:

The heart is deceitful above all things, and desperately
wicked; who can know it?[105]

Jeremiah tells us the truth. The human heart is indeed sinful and wicked. Human nature proves this beyond all doubt. Then what can our Lord mean by an "honest and good heart: It means one knows he is wrong and that he has sinned against God. But by the grace of God he confesses his sin to God. When a man does that he is an honest man before God. When a man realizes his sinful condition then God can help. There are many people today who are lost in sin. The Bible teaches that in the last days many would follow after the lies of Satan. We are living in those days now. It is only a matter of time before Jesus Christ the Son of God returns to this world. On that great day our Savior will end the rebellion of this world.

Throughout the scripture we read where God invites men to come to Him. God is gracious and will forgive all manner of sin. But so many would rather heed the voice of Satan. This reminds us of our Lord's words recorded in Matthew 7:13.

> *Enter in at the straight gate; for wide is the gate and broad is the way, that leadeth to destruction, and many there be who go that way; because strait is the gate, and narrow is the way, which leadeth unto life, and few there be that find it.*[106]

Thank God there are some that find that better way. Our Lord describes these in this parable of the sower. The seed on this hearer is, on, down, and up with much fruit being produced. Matthew records something else about this person. Some bring forth thirty-fold fruit, some sixty and some a hundred. The thirty expresses the lowest degree of fruitfulness; the sixty is much better. These are really doing something for God.

But behold the hundred-fold, the highest degree. How many are bringing forth a hundred-fold for Jesus. We need to be honest with ourselves. What type of person are we? What type of person do we want to be? The Bible tells us: II Corinthians 13:5

> *Examine yourselves, whether you are in the faith; prove yourselves. Know ye are not yourselves how Jesus Christ is in you, unless you are discredited.*[107]

God expects each of us to examine ourselves. He expects all His people to worship and love Him. All believers should find a Bible believing Church and worship God with other believers.

Chapter XV

God's Charis

Our God delights to show grace to sinners! The Pharisees held this against our Lord from the beginning of His ministry. They had no interest for the despised and outcast of society. But the heart of our Savior went out to those that were lost and despised. Jesus came not to call the righteous, but sinners to repentance.

Our Scripture for this lesson is taken from the" Book of Luke 7:36-50.

> And one of the Pharisees desired him that he would eat with him. And he went into the Pharisee's house, and sat down to eat. And, behold, a woman in the city, who was a sinner, when she knew that Jesus was eating in the Pharisee's house, brought an alabaster box of ointment, and stood at His feet behind Him, weeping; and began to wash his feet with tears, and did wipe them with the hair of her head, and kissed his feet, and anointed them with ointment. Now when the Pharisee who had bidden him saw it, he spoke within himself saying, this man, if he were a prophet, would have known who and what manner of woman this is that toucheth him; for she is a sinner. And Jesus answering, said unto him, Simon, I have something to say unto thee. And he saith, Master, say on. There was certain creditor who had two debtors: the one owed five hundred pence, and the other fifty. And

when they had nothing to pay, he frankly forgave them both. Tell me, therefore, which of them will love him most? Simon answered, and said, I suppose that he to whom the forgave most. And he said unto him, thou hast rightly judged. And he turned to the woman, and said unto Simon, seest thou this woman? I entered into thine house; thou gavest no water for my feet. But she hath washed my feet with tears, and wiped them with the hair of her head. Thou gavest me no kiss. But this woman, since the time I came in, hath not ceased to kiss my feet. My head with oil thou didst not anoint. But this woman hath anointed my feet with ointment. Wherefore, I say unto thee, her sins, which are many, are forgiven; for she loved much. But to whom little is forgiven, the same loveth little. And he said unto her, thy sins are forgiven. And they that were eating with him began to say within themselves, who is that forgiveth sins also? And he said to the woman, thy faith hath saved thee; go in peace.[108]

As our Lord Jesus sat eating in the home of the Pharisee a great crowd began to gather. Right outside the door a poor sinful woman was looking in. The Scripture says that she was a sinner. No doubt her life was one of deep moral sin and misery. She was in bondage to Satan and sin. She had no character and was despised by everyone and yet she wanted to see Jesus and seek relief for her burden of sin. Her heart was troubled and she long for the cleansing power of God. She was an immoral person. She sold her body for a few pennies. Her life was wasting away in sin. All through the ages respectable people have looked down on her kind. These people are still looked down on. Many Churches today would not want this type of woman to visit them. We need to remember what the Word of God teaches. Paul writes in Romans that: Romans 3:23.

For all have sinned, and come short of the glory of God.[109]

The Apostle also writes: Romans 1:10.

As it is written, there is none righteous, no not one.[110]

This is a fact that some Christians seem to forget. All of us are in need of the Savior. We also need to remember that there never was a fallen woman unless some man has caused her this immoral condition. Often the one who causes this condition in the woman is accepted as a good member of society. Jesus said that publicans and harlots would go into the kingdom of heaven before the hard-hearted Pharisees.

Perhaps this sinful woman had heard Jesus preach. How her heart must have cried out when she heard the Savior say, "Come unto me, all ye that labor and are heavy laden, and I will give you rest. Take my yoke upon you, and learn of me; for I am meek and lowly in heart, and ye shall find rest unto your souls. For my yoke is easy, and my burden is light (Matthew 11: 28-30)."

The woman could not stay away any longer. She burst into the room and fell at Jesus' feet. Realizing her need of cleansing she began to wash Jesus' feet with her tears and to dry with her beautiful hair. She wiped His feet with that lovely hair that had perhaps lured others to her house of shame. Now she was washing the feet of Jesus with her tears and drying them with her lovely hair. She began to kiss His feet. The Pharisee thought in his heart how can this man be a prophet and not know this woman is a sinner. I wonder how the Pharisee knew her so well! He knew her character. He knew the life she had lived. Perhaps he had spent some time in private with her. Perhaps he had helped contribute to her sinful condition. Loose morality among professing Christians is nothing new. It has been around since the beginning of time. The Pharisee would have nothing to do with her in public. He thought in his heart that he was better than her. This man was deceiving himself.

Thank God, Jesus did not turn us away when he come to Him in faith. He knew this woman was a sinner. That is why He welcomed her. Jesus came to redeem sinners. Jesus said in the book of Luke 19:10.

> For the Son of Man is come to seek and to save that which was lost.[111]

It rejoices the heart of God when sinners come to Him is faith. Today Christ Jesus stands ready to forgive and receive all those who come to Him in simple faith.

As one reads the Bible he never ceases to wonder at the amazing grace of God. God's grace is beyond human imagination. This is especially true when we consider the doctrine on sanctification.

Paul writes in many places concerning the grace of God. His words to the Colossians brings much comfort to the hearts of believers today. The Apostle writes: Colossians 1:12.

> Giving thanks unto the Father, who hath made us fit to be partakers of the inheritance of the saints in light.[112]

This verse tells us that God has made us fit for heaven now! The pastor\counselor should ever keep this important truth before God's people. People need to know the truth concerning their relationship with Jesus Christ. The saved of this world have a special relationship to Christ Jesus. We have been brought with His precious blood. At the moment of salvation God makes us perfect in Him. Paul writes: 5: 8-11.

> But God commendeth his love toward us in that, while we are yet sinners, Christ died for us. Much more then, being now justified by His blood, we shall be saved from wrath through Him. For if, when were enemies, we were reconciled to God by the death of His Son, much more, being reconciled, we shall be saved by His life.[113]

Our salvation is complete at the moment of conversion. There is nothing we must do to improve on the work of God in our hearts. We are saved by the blood of Jesus Christ through faith in Him.

There is terrible heresy in this world. It teaches that when God saves a sinner, the sinner must then make himself fit for heaven. The Bible teaches no such thing! This does not mean that the believer does not grow in grace, for we do. When a sinner is saved he becomes a babe in Christ. Through prayer and the study of God's Word the believer grows in Christ.

However, the moment a person is saved he is fit for heaven. We are sanctified by the Holy Spirit of God. The word "sanctified" means that we have been set apart by God. Notice the grace of God as recorded in Hebrews 10:14.

For by one offering he hath perfected forever them that are sanctified.[114]

This verse not only teaches that we are fit for heaven at conversion; it also teaches the eternal security of the believer. The Apostle Peter sheds much light on this subject. The Apostle writes: I Peter 2:9.

But ye are a chosen generation, a royal priesthood, an holy nation, a peculiar people, that ye should show forth the praises of him who called you out of darkness into His marvelous light.[115]

This verse is not talking about some time in the future in the life of the believer. It speaks of the present. Notice again the believer's position in Christ. (1) You are chosen. (2) You are a royal priesthood. (3) You are peculiar people or rather the people of God.

This verse is indeed a sacred jewel from the riches of God's treasure. The believer is special to God. Because of this we should forever praise the name of God. There are many saints living in the cemetery of doubts and fear, not claiming the promises of God. They are standing on the shores of the Jordan looking over in the Promised Land. God's people need to cross over Jordan into the Beulah land, and walk with God. Some may say, but we don't have the strength, patience or courage. We cannot cross alone. God does not expect us to cross alone. He holds out His hand today as He did to the Peter two thousand years ago. The believer is held in the hands of God. He is our protector and shield. Our life does not depend upon our power and strength. Note the Word of God as recorded by the prophet Zechariah 4:6.

Then he answered and spoke unto me, saying, this is the Word of the Lord unto Zerubabel, saying, not by might, not by power, but by my Spirit, saith the Lord of hosts.[116]

The Scripture tells us much about the grace of God. God's grace bestows pleasure and delight on the believer. God's grace can change the heart of the hardest criminal. The grace of God can make the cold blooded killer into an angel of light. There is a wonderful transforming power in the grace of God.

There are two men mentioned in I Corinthians chapter one that has touched by the grace of God. The first mentioned is the Apostle Paul. We know more about this man than perhaps any other in Scripture. God used this once great sinner in a mighty way. The Holy Spirit used this man to write fourteen books of the New Testament. I believe that Paul wrote the Book of Hebrews.

We find Paul first mentioned in Acts 7:58. Here he is referred to by his Jewish name Saul. Saul was a great enemy of or Lord Jesus Christ. His great goal in life was to stamp out the Church of the living God. Saul hated the very name of Jesus.

Saul was standing by when Steven was stoned to death for preaching the good news of Jesus. Steven was a deacon full of the Holy Ghost. Steven was brought before the Sanhedrin for preaching the Gospel of Christ. Steven's message in Acts chapter seven began with Abraham and ended with Christ Jesus. There is no greater name than Jesus. There is no Name under heaven whereby men may be saved. We live in a day of cults and false religions, where millions deny the Lord Jesus Christ as the Eternal Son of God. There is coming a day when all men will bow at the Name of Jesus, and confess Him as Lord, to the glory of God. Paul was moved by the Holy Spirit to write: Philippians 2: 10, 11.

> Wherefore, God also hath highly exalted him, and given Him a name which is above every name, that at the name of Jesus every knee should bow, of things in heaven, and things in earth, and things under the earth, and that every tongue should confess that Jesus Christ is Lord, to the glory of God the Father.[117]

Steven's message was to much for the Sanhedrin. His message cut them to the heart. The Bible says that they gnashed on him with their teeth. The word "gnash" means to bite, or to eat greedily. The Word of God will always have an effect on those who hear. Men will either accept or reject the Word of God. Paul writes in Hebrews 4:12.

> For the Word of God is quick, and powerful, and shaper than any two-edged sword, piercing even to the dividing

asunder of soul and spirit, and of the joints and marrow, and
is a discerner of the thoughts and intents of the heart.[118]

The Jewish leaders took Steven out and murdered him for preaching the cross of Christ Jesus. Saul was there to consent to Steven's death. He gave his approval as this man of God was killed. From that day on Saul became the number one enemy of Satan. He went everywhere persecuting the Church of God.

God's grace and mercy can change even the heart of a wicked Saul. Saul was on the way to Damascus to persecute more Christians. On this trip he met the Savior Himself. A great light appeared and Saul was cast to the ground blinded. God opened this great sinner's heart! Saul heard the voice of Jesus, saying, "Saul, Saul, why persecutest thou me (Acts 9:4)." Saul's eyes were opened; this great enemy of the faith was brought into the kingdom of God.

The other man touched by the grace of God was Sosthenes. We know little about this man. He was the chief ruler of the synagogue at Corinth (Acts 18:17). He to was an enemy of Christ who was converted from his sins.

Yes, the grace of God can change the heart of man. The Bible is filled with the names of sinners who were touched by the hand of God Today; churches are filled with people who had their sins forgiven. We rejoice knowing that our names are written in the Lamb's Book of Life. God is offering His grace today. Peter wrote long ago: II Peter 3:9.

The Lord is not slack concerning His promise, as some
men count slackness, but is longsuffering toward us, not
willing that any should perish, but that all should come to
repentance.[119]

As we conclude our study on the grace of God we need to consider Paul's words to the Romans. Romans 5:8 is one of the most precious verses in the Bible. Paul writes:

But God commendeth his love toward us in that, while we
were yet sinners, Christ died for us.[120]

Every believer knows of the matchless grace of our God. Romans 3:23 teaches that all men have sinned and come short of the glory of God. Jeremiah the prophet of old knew will of the condition of the human heart. As this man of God was being persecuted for faith in proclaiming the Word of God he cried out: Jeremiah 17:9.

> The heart is deceitful above all things, and desperately wicked; who can know it?[121]

This verse reminds us of the heart felt feelings of King David when he confessed: Psalm 51:5.

> Behold, I was shaped in iniquity, and in sin did my mother conceive me.[122]

Everyone who comes to the loving arms of God realizes his great in and a need for the Savior. One of the greatest blessings of God's grace is the fact that when the sinner is saved God remembers his sins and iniquities no more. God declares in the Book of Hebrews 10:16, 17.

> This is the covenant that I will make them after those days, saith the Lord: I will put my laws into their hearts, and in their minds will I write them, and their sins and iniquities will I remember no more.[123]

This is hard for many to understand. God's grace is eternal and perfect. When sinners by simple faith put their trust in the finished work of Christ, God forgives and saves.

Paul writes a long list of sins in the Book of Corinthians. The Apostle writes: I Corinthians 6: 9-11.

> Know ye not that the unrighteous shall not inherit the kingdom of God? Be not deceived: neither fornicators, nor idolaters, not adulterers, nor effeminate, nor abusers of themselves with mankind, nor thieves, nor covetous, nor drunkards, nor revilers, nor extortioners, shall inherit the kingdom of God. And such were some of you; but you are washed, but ye are

sanctified, but ye are justified in the name of the Lord Jesus, and by the Spirit of our God.[124]

Most all people at one time or another have committed some sins. We read these verses with trembling and fear knowing that we have sinned against God. Thank God for verse eleven. It deserves to be read again! I Corinthians 6:11.

And such were some of you, but ye are washed, but ye are sanctified, but ye are justified in the name of the Lord Jesus, and by the Spirit of our God.[125]

John Newton who wrote "Amazing Grace" must have been thinking about this verse of Scripture when he cried out from his death bed, "I am a great sinner but I have a great Savior." This reminds us of the words of Paul when he cried out: Romans 7:24.

Oh wretched man that I am! We shall deliver me from this body of death.[126]

Paul was a great man of God but he had the same struggles that we have. The seventh chapter of Romans opens up the heart of this man of God. The believer today finds his answer of hope and peace in the same Savior that Paul did two thousand years ago. Note again our verse in Romans 5:8.

But God commendeth his love toward us in that, while we were yet sinners, Christ died for us.[127]

Man cannot save himself. Only God can change a man's heart of stone. There are so many today we think they can save themselves. They are being deceived by Satan to trust in their good name or works. This verse teaches that Jesus died for sinners. This is the greatest love the world has ever known. Only God can commend this type of love. The believer does not lightly his great salvation. It is true that eternal life is free to all those who receive Christ as Savior. Our blessed Lord Himself declares: Revelation 22: 16, 17.

I, Jesus, have sent mine angel to testify unto you these things in the churches. I am the root and the offspring of David, and the bright and morning star. And the Spirit and the bride say, come. And let him that is athirst come. And whosoever will, let him take the water of life freely.[128]

Yes, our salvation is a free gift from God. But there was a great cost! This great salvation that we have cost God the death of Jesus Christ His only beloved Son on the Roman cross. The Christian Minister\ Counselor has much to offer the people of this world. We have the words of life from the Creator Himself. God has given us His Word that we may come to know Him. It is through His Word and the ministry of the Holy Spirit that we are able to face the trials and temptations of this life. We have the blessed assurance that Christ Jesus will always be with is in us. However, we all claim that wonderful prayer of John the Apostle, when he cried out: Revelation 22:20:

Even so, come, Lord Jesus.[129]

CHAPTER XVI

Homosexuality And LESBIANISM & BEASTITALITY

The Holy Bible teaches us that homosexuality is a serious, depraved sin, that Almighty God hates, passionately. Since this is God's stance against this type of sin, behavior and lifestyle lived by such a large population in our society, today. It must be stated here and be understood, that God, did not create this character trait, make up or mentality in the human being population. It must be further understood, that homosexuality and lesbianism are indeed, learned experiences/behaviors. Said behaviors are strongly condemned by God. Homosexuality and lesbianism are undoubtably within the top most hated sins by God. In God's mercy and grace, He warns against becoming involved in said behaviors and lifestyles.

In the Old Testament of God's Holy Bible, God destroyed an entire city, (Sodom-Gomarrah), because of homosexuality. Homosexuality and lesbianism are perverted sins, as it is a sin against natural affections of a man and/or woman. We see this taught clearly in the Book of Romans 1:26, 27.

> For this cause God gave them up unto vile affections: for even Their women did change the natural use into that which is against nature. And likewise also the men, leaving the natural use of woman, burned in their lust one toward another men with men working that which is unseemly, and receiving in themselves that recompence of their error which was meet.

Therefore, God warns against people and society becoming involved in homosexuality and lesbianism. If people fail to heed the warning cited in Romans, they will not only receive eternal damnation in the second death (hell & the lake of fire), but will also receive physical and mental punishment in present evil world, through their bodies and minds in this life.

In Africa, (considered by a standard, to be a third world country), might be considered by most societies, to be a primitive culture. However, if a person is found guilty of homosexuality or lesbianism, the convicted parties, maybe sentenced to death. Also, the Muslim religion condemns homosexuality and lesbianism. The convicted offenders maybe put to death.

Again in Genesis is where the origin of homosexuality is gleamed. Genesis 19:5.

> And they (men of the city), called unto Lot, and said unto him where are the men, (angels)? Which came in to thee this night? Bring them out to us, that we may know (have sex with) them.

However, in America certain politicians and government officials not only recognize homosexuality and lesbianism, as an acceptable behavior and lifestyle, but also embraces it to the extent of allowing unions, partnerships, same sex marriages in a number of States within the United States of America. America has allowed homosexuals and lesbians the rights under the tendents of human and civil rights. Further, go so far to allow these people the rights to purchase healthcare for their sex partners.

People who practice homosexuality and lesbianism, feel like they are right and have the right to do so. They feel safe and acceptable in this lifestyle before God and the public. They are sadly misinformed. They are in fact condemned before God and the devout Christians who practice the true teaching of God and His Son-Christ Jesus. They (homosexuals / lesbians) will not enter God's Heaven, unless they confess and repent these sins unto Christ. They will without a doubt go to a devils hell and have eternity to regret not turning from this lifestyle.

We will now look closer at the Holy Scriptures which actually teach and warn against becoming involved with homosexuality and lesbianism: Deuteronomy 23:17.

> There shall be no whore of the daughters of Israel, nor A
> sodomite of the sons of Israel.

Now, we see another dimension given, not only are men forbidden to lie down men with men and women with women. God says, we are not to have sex with animals either. Leviticus 18:22, 23, 24.

> Thou shalt not lie with mankind, as with womankind;
> It is abomination. Neither shalt thou lie with any beast
> To defile thyself therewith; neither shall any woman
> Stand before a beast to down thereto; it is confusion.
> Defile not ye yourselves in any of these things: for in
> All these the nations are defiled which I cast out before you.

Bibliography

Adams, Jay E. The Christians Counselors Manual. Grand Rapids: Zondervan Publishing House, 1973

Adams, Jay E. A Theology Of Christian Counseling. Grand Rapids: Zondervan Publishing, 1979

Collins, Gary. Christian Counseling: A Comprehensive Guide Waco. Word Books, 1980

Crabb, Lawrence. Basic Principles of Counseling. Grand Rapids: Zondervan Publishing, 1973

Crabb, Lawrence. Effective Biblical Counseling. Zondervan Publishing House, 1977

Drakefore, John Counseling For Church Leaders. Nashville: Broadman Press, 1970

Hamilton, James. The Mystery of Pastoral Counseling. Grand Rapids: Baker

Meir, Paul. Introduction To Psychology And Counseling. Grand Rapids: Baker, 1982

Minirth, Frank. Christian Psychiatry. Old Tappan: Fleming H. Revell Company, 1977

Minirth, Frank and Meier, Paul. <u>Happiness Is A Choice.</u> Grand Rapids: Baker 1978

Narramore, Clyde. <u>Encyclopedia Of Psychological Problems.</u> Grand Rapids: Zondervan Publishing House, 1961

Narramore, Clyde. <u>The Psychology Of Counseling.</u> Grand Rapids: Zondervan Publishing House, 1957

Narramore, Clyde. <u>You're Someone Special.</u> Grand Rapids: Grand Rapids: Zondervan Publishing House, 1969

Oates, Wayne. <u>Pastoral Counseling.</u> Philadelphia: Westminister Press, 1974

Solomon, Charles. <u>Counseling With The Mind Of Christ.</u> Old Tappan: Fleming H. Revell Company, 1977

Tournier, Paul. <u>Guilt And Grace: A Psychological Study.</u> New York: Harper and Row, 1957

Wagner, Maurice. <u>Put It All Together.</u> Grand Rapids: Zondervan Publishing House, 1976

We recommend, very highly, Dr. Frey's book, "God Oriented Perspective On Counseling and Applied Psychology." Dr. Frey is qualified by both Academic Achievements and Clinical Practice to produce this outstanding work. We plan to make it available to our students here at Triune Biblical University.

President
Leroy Mikels, Th. D.

Chaplain/Lt. General Bob H. Frey, LLD JCD LJL, and his wife Deborah maintain homes in both Jonesboro and Lyons, Georgia. Deborah is a graduate of Brewton-Parker College and Tift College of Mercer University. Dr. Frey is a Canon Lawyer & Counselor and member of the North American Canon Law Society and member: National Lawyers Association.

His academic achievements are as follows:

Dr. of Philosophy in Christian Counseling, Ph.D. American Bible College & Seminary

Dr. of Canonical Jurisprudence, JCD, Romano Byzantine College

Dr. of Religious Education; Master of Arts in Theology; Bachelor of Arts in Religious Education all from Immanuel Baptist Theological Seminary.

Dr. of Philosophy in Sociology, Ph.D., Columbia Pacific University

Dr. of Bible Philosophy, International Seminary.

Dr. of Sacred Laws and Letters (Honorary), L.L.D., Christian Bible College

Dr. of Divinity, (Honorary) Romano Byzantine College.

Dr. of Education in Counseling and Administration, Ed.D., Immanuel Baptist Seminary

Master of Arts in Counseling, Luther Rice Seminary.

Endnotes

[1]   John 14:6

[2]   Adams E. Jay, <u>The Christian Counselors Manual</u> (Grand Rapids: Zondervan Publishing House, 1973) p. 5

[3]   Galatians 3: 3

[4]   Matthew 11: 28-30

[5]   Spurgeon H. Charles, <u>Lectures To My Students</u> (Grand Rapids: Zondervan Publishing House, 1954)

[6]   Hebrews 4: 12

[7]   II Timothy 3: 16-17

[8]   Adams E. Jay, <u>The Christian Counselors Manual</u> (Grand Rapids: Zondervan Publishing House, 1973) p. 322

[9]   Isaiah 1: 18

[10]   John 8: 44

[11]   Ibid., p. 250

[12]   Ibid., p. 49

[13]   James 5: 16

[14]   Ibid., p. 50

[15]   Frank B. Minirth and Paul D. Meir, <u>Happiness Is A Choice</u> (Grand Rapids: Baker Book House, 1978) p. 79

[16]   Ephesians 5: 22-33 - 6: 1-4

[17]   Matthew 19: 5-6

[18]   Matthew 19: 9

[19]   I Corinthians 6: 15-18

[20]   John 2: 1,2

[21]   I Corinthians 7: 11

[22]   Matthew 19: 9

[23]   I Corinthians 7: 14

24 Genesis 13: 1-8

25 Malachi 2: 14-15

26 I Corinthians 7: 15

27 Jay E. Adams, The Christian Counselors Manual (Grand Rapids: Zondervan Publishing House, 1973) p. 61-62

28 Gary R Collins, Christian Counseling, A Comprehensive Guide (Waco: Word Books, 1980) p. 282

29 Jay E. Adams, The Christian Counselors Manual (Grand Rapids: Zondervan Publishing House, 1973) p. 392

30 I Corinthians 6: 13-18

31 I Corinthians 7: 9

32 Genesis 2: 18

33 II Samuel 16: 21-22

34 Ephesians 6: 12

35 I John 2: 9

36 Gary R Collins, Christian Counseling, A Comprehensive Guide (Waco: Word Books, 1980) p. 288

37 Romans 1: 24, 27-29

38 Romans 8: 9

39 Ibid., p. 290

40 James 4: 7

41 Genesis 3: 15

42 Genesis 3: 1

43 Luke 21: 19

44 Zephaniah 3: 5-7

45 Revelation 1: 1

46 Matthew 2: 16-18

47 Mark 13: 20

48 Philippians 2: 9-11

49 John 12: 8

50 I Peter 3: 17

51 Habakkuk 3: 17-19

52 Philippians 4: 11-13

53 Romans 16: 17-18

54 Matthew 6: 28-34

55 Luke 9: 5

56 Colossians 2: 4-6

57 Habakkuk 3: 18

58   Matthew 11: 28-30
59   I Peter 5: 7
60   Matthew 11: 28-30
61   I John 3: 13
62   I Peter 3: 14-17
63   Luke 7: 21-23
64   Ephesians 2: 8,9
65   Luke 12: 28,29
66   Genesis 12: 1-3
67   I Peter 1: 7
68   Genesis 12: 12
69   Genesis 20: 12
70   Genesis 26: 7
71   Genesis 12: 18, 19
72   Acts 3: 6
73   Matthew 24: 6,7
74   Ephesians 6: 12-17
75   Hebrews 2: 10
76   Exodus 14: 14
77   Romans 7: 15-25, The Living Bible
78   John 3: 3
79   Romans 8: 9
80   John 14: 23
81   Galatians 5: 16
82   Mark 3: 22-29
83   Hebrews 2: 14
84   I John 3: 8
85   I John 5: 18
86   Gary R Collins, Christian Counseling, A Comprehensive Guide (Waco: Word Books, 1980) p.72
87   Genesis 2: 18
88   Matthew 27: 46
89   Job 25: 6
90   Psalm 22: 6
91   Hebrews 4: 15
92   Psalm 25: 16
93   Ecclesiastes 8: 6
94   Romans 12: 1-2

95 Matthew 13: 1-23
96 Ecclesiastes 11: 6
97 I Peter 1: 23
98 Isaiah 55: 11
99 John 5: 24
100 Jeremiah 4: 3
101 II Timothy 4: 1-2
102 Luke 8: 10
103 Deuteronomy 32: 39
104 Luke 8: 15
105 Jeremiah 17: 9
106 Matthew 7: 13
107 II Corinthians 13: 5
108 Luke 7: 36-50
109 Romans 3: 23
110 Romans 1: 10
111 Luke 19: 10
112 Colossians 1: 12
113 Romans 5: 8-11
114 Hebrews 10: 14
115 I Peter 2: 9
116 Zechariah 4: 6
117 Philippians 2: 10-11
118 Hebrews 4: 12
119 II Peter 3: 9
120 Romans 5: 8
121 Jeremiah 17: 9
122 Psalm 51: 5
123 Hebrews 10: 16-17
124 I Corinthians 6: 9-11
125 I Corinthians 6: 11
126 Romans 7: 24
127 Romans 5: 8
128 Revelation 22: 16-17
129 Revelation 22: 30

www.ingramcontent.com/pod-product-compliance
Lightning Source LLC
Chambersburg PA
CBHW020306290526
45784CB00003B/1388